MICROSOFT OFFICE 4
FOR WINDOWS FOR
DUMMIES™

Quick Reference

by Doug Lowe

IDG BOOKS

IDG Books Worldwide, Inc.
An International Data Group Company

Foster City, CA ♦ Chicago, IL ♦ Indianapolis, IN ♦ Braintree, MA ♦ Dallas, TX

Microsoft Office 4 For Windows For Dummies
Quick Reference

Published by
IDG Books Worldwide, Inc.
An International Data Group Company
919 E. Hillsdale Blvd.
Suite 400
Foster City, CA 94404

Library of Congress Catalog Card No.: 94-79606

ISBN: 1-56884-958-3

Printed in the United States of America

10 9 8 7 6 5 4 3 2

1A/QZ/RS/ZU

Distributed in the United States by IDG Books Worldwide, Inc.

Distributed in Canada by Macmillan of Canada, a Division of Canada Publishing Corporation; by Computer and Technical Books in Miami, Florida, for South America and the Caribbean; by Longman Singapore in Singapore, Malaysia, Thailand, and Korea; by Toppan Co. Ltd. in Japan; by Asia Computerworld in Hong Kong; by Woodslane Pty. Ltd. in Australia and New Zealand; and by Transworld Publishers Ltd. in the U.K. and Europe.

For general information on IDG Books in the U.S., including information on discounts and premiums, contact IDG Books 800-434-3422 or 415-312-0650.

For information on where to purchase IDG Books outside the U.S., contact Christina Turner at 415-312-0650.

For information on translations, contact Marc Jeffrey Mikulich, Director, Foreign & Subsidiary Rights, at IDG Books Worldwide, 415-312-0650.

For sales inquiries and special prices for bulk quantities, write to the address above or call IDG Books Worldwide at 415-312-0650.

For information on using IDG Books in the classroom, or for ordering examination copies, contact Jim Kelly at 800-434-2086.

is a registered trademark of
IDG Books Worldwide, Inc.

About the Author

Doug Lowe has written more than 15 computer books, including IDG's *Networking For Dummies* and *PowerPoint 4 For Windows For Dummies,* and knows how to present boring technostuff in a style that is both entertaining and enlightening. He is a contributing editor to IDG's *DOS Resource Guide*.

Acknowledgments

First of all, to Pam Mourouzis: Thanks for sticking with me and this project through thick and thin, for not chewing me out for missing deadlines, and for whipping everything into shape. To Michael Simsic and Michael Partington: Thanks for your editorial and technical contributions in making this book both readable and accurate. To Diane Steele: Thanks for providing that overall vision that helped set this book on course and for gently providing those necessary mid-course corrections. And to San Mateoan Megg Bonar: Thanks for getting this project going, for encouraging me along the way, and for not changing your phone number.

(The publisher would like to thank Patrick J. McGovern, without whom this book would not have been possible.)

iv

ABOUT IDG BOOKS WORLDWIDE

WINNER
Eighth Annual Computer Press Awards 1992

WINNER
Ninth Annual Computer Press Awards 1993

Welcome to the world of IDG Books Worldwide.

IDG Books Worldwide, Inc. is a subsidiary of International Data Group, the world's largest publisher of computer-related information and the leading global provider of information services on information technology. IDG was founded more than 25 years ago and now employs more than 7,000 people worldwide. IDG publishes more than 220 computer publications in 65 countries (see listing below). More than fifty million people read one or more IDG publications each month.

Launched in 1990, IDG Books Worldwide is today the #1 publisher of best-selling computer books in the United States. We are proud to have received 3 awards from the Computer Press Association in recognition of editorial excellence, and our best-selling ...For Dummies™ series has more than 12 million copies in print with translations in 25 languages. IDG Books, through a recent joint venture with IDG's Hi-Tech Beijing, became the first U.S. publisher to publish computer book in the People's Republic of China. In record time, IDG Books has become the first choice for millions of readers around the world who want to learn how to better manage their businesses.

Our mission is simple: Every IDG book is designed to bring extra value and skill-building instructions to the reader. Our books are written by experts who understand and care about our readers. The knowledge base of our editorial staff comes from years of experience in publishing, education, and journalism — experience which we use to produce books for the '90s. In short, we care about books, so we attract the best people. We devote special attention to details such as audience, interior design, use of icons, and illustrations. And because we use an efficient process of authoring, editing, and desktop publishing our books electronically, we can spend more time ensuring superior content and spend less time on the technicalities of making books.

You can count on our commitment to deliver high-quality books at competitive prices on topics consumers want to read about. At IDG, we value quality, and we have been delivering quality for more than 25 years. You'll find no better book on a subject than an IDG book.

John J. Kilcullen

John Kilcullen
President and CEO
IDG Books Worldwide, Inc.

IDG Books Worldwide, Inc. is a subsidiary of International Data Group, the world's largest publisher of computer-related information and the leading global provider of information services on information technology. International Data Group publishes over 220 computer publications in 65 countries. More than fifty million people read one or more International Data Group publications each month. The officers are Patrick J. McGovern, Founder and Board Chairman; Kelly Conlin, President; Jim Casella, Chief Operating Officer. International Data Group's publications include: ARGENTINA'S Computerworld Argentina, Infoworld Argentina; AUSTRALIA'S Computerworld Australia, Computer Living, Australian PC World, Australian Macworld, Network World, Mobile Business Australia, Publish!, Reseller, IDG Sources; AUSTRIA'S Computerwelt Oesterreich, PC Test; BELGIUM'S Data News (CW); BOLIVIA'S Computerworld; BRAZIL'S Computerworld, Connections, Game Power, Mundo Unix, PC World, Publish, Super Game; BULGARIA'S Computerworld Bulgaria, PC & Mac World Bulgaria, Network World Bulgaria; CANADA'S CIO Canada, Computerworld Canada, InfoCanada, Network World Canada, Reseller; CHILE'S Computerworld Chile, Informatica; COLOMBIA'S Computerworld Colombia, PC World; COSTA RICA'S PC World; CZECH REPUBLIC'S Computerworld Elektronika, PC World; DENMARK'S Communications World, Computerworld Danmark, Computerworld Focus, Macintosh Produktkatalog, Macworld Danmark, PC World Danmark, PC Produktguide, Tech World, Windows World; ECUADOR'S PC World Ecuador; EGYPT'S Computerworld (CW) Middle East, PC World Middle East; FINLAND'S MikroPC, Tietoviikko, Tietoverkko; FRANCE'S Distributique, GOLDEN MAC, InfoPC, Le Guide du Monde Informatique, Le Monde Informatique, Telecoms & Reseaux; GERMANY'S Computerwoche, Computerwoche Focus, Computerwoche Extra, Electronic Entertainment, Gamepro, Information Management, Macwelt, Netzwelt, PC Welt, Publish, Publish; GREECE'S Publish & Macworld; HONG KONG'S Computerworld Hong Kong, PC World Hong Kong; HUNGARY'S Computerworld SZT, PC World; INDIA'S Computers & Communications; INDONESIA'S Info Komputer; IRELAND'S ComputerScope; ISRAEL'S Beyond Windows, Computerworld Israel, Multimedia, PC World Israel; ITALY'S Computerworld Italia, Lotus Magazine, Macworld Italia, Networking Italia, PC Shopping Italy, PC World Italia; JAPAN'S Computerworld Today, Information Systems World, Macworld Japan, Nikkei Personal Computing, SunWorld Japan, Windows World; KENYA'S East African Computer News; KOREA'S Computerworld Korea, Macworld Korea, PC World Korea; LATIN AMERICA'S GamePro; MALAYSIA'S Computerworld Malaysia, PC World Malaysia; MEXICO'S Compu Edicion, Compu Manufactura, Computacion/Punto de Venta, Computerworld Mexico, MacWorld, Mundo Unix, PC World, Windows; THE NETHERLAND'S Computer! Totaal, Computable (CW), LAN Magazine, Lotus Magazine, MacWorld; NEW ZEALAND'S Computer Buyer, Computerworld New Zealand, Network World, New Zealand PC World; NIGERIA'S PC World Africa; NORWAY'S Computerworld Norge, Lotusworld Norge, Macworld Norge, Maxi Data, Networld, PC World Ekspress, PC World Nettverk, PC World Norge, PC World's Produktguide, Publish& Multimedia World, Student Data, Unix World, Windowsworld; PAKISTAN'S PC World Pakistan; PANAMA'S PC World Panama; PERU'S Computerworld Peru, PC World; PEOPLE'S REPUBLIC OF CHINA'S China Computerworld, China Infoworld, China PC Info Magazine, Computer Fan, PC World China, Electronics International, Electronics Today/Multimedia World, Electronic Product World, China Network World, Software World Magazine, Telecom Product World; PHILIPPINES' Computerworld Philippines, PC Digest (PCW); POLAND'S Computerworld Poland, Computerworld Special Report, Networld, PC World/Komputer, Sunworld; PORTUGAL'S Cerebro/PC World, Correio Informatico/Computerworld, MacIn; ROMANIA'S Computerworld, PC World, Telecom Romania; RUSSIA'S Computerworld-Moscow, Mir - PK (PCW), Sety (Networks); SINGAPORE'S Computerworld Southeast Asia, PC World Singapore; SLOVENIA'S Monitor Magazine; SOUTH AFRICA'S Computer Mail (CIO), Computing S.A. ,Network World S.A., Software World; SPAIN'S Advanced Systems, Amiga World, Computerworld Espana, Communicaciones World, Macworld Espana, NeXTWORLD, Super Juegos Magazine (GamePro), PC World Espana, Publish; SWEDEN'S Attack, ComputerSweden, Corporate Computing, Macworld, Mikrodatorn, Natverk & Kommunikation, PC World, CAP & Design, Datalngenjoren, Maxi Data,Windows World; SWITZERLAND'S Computerworld Schweiz, Macworld Schweiz, PC Tip; TAIWAN'S Computerworld Taiwan, PC World Taiwan; THAILAND'S Thai Computerworld; TURKEY'S Computerworld Monitor, Macworld Turkiye, PC World Turkiye; UKRAINE'S Computerworld Computers+Software Magazine; UNITED KINGDOM'S Computing /Computerworld, Connexion/Network World, Lotus Magazine, Macworld, Open Computing/Sunworld; URUGUAY'S PC World Uruguay; UNITED STATES' Advanced Systems, AmigaWorld, Cable in the Classroom, CD Review, CIO, Computerworld, Computerworld Client/Server Journal, Digital Video, DOS World, Electronic Entertainment Magazine (E2), Federal Computer Week, Game Hits, GamePro, IDG Books, Infoworld, Laser Event, Macworld, Maximize, Multimedia World, Network World, PC Letter, PC World, Publish, SWATPro, Video Event; VENEZUELA'S Computerworld Venezuela, PC World; VIETNAM'S PC World Vietnam.
11-16-9

Credits

Executive VP, Strategic Product Planning & Research
David Solomon

Editorial Director
Diane Graves Steele

Acquisitions Editor
Megg Bonar

Brand Manager
Judith A. Taylor

Editorial Managers
Tracy L. Barr
Sandra Blackthorn

Editorial Assistants
Tamara S. Castleman
Stacey Holden Prince
Kevin Spencer

Acquisitions Assistant
Suki Gear

Production Director
Beth Jenkins

Associate Project Coordinator
Valery Bourke

Pre-Press Coordinator
Steve Peake

Editors
Pamela Mourouzis
Michael Simsic

Technical Reviewer
Michael J. Partington

Production Staff
Tony Augsburger
Chris Collins
Mark Owens
Dwight Ramsey
Patricia R. Reynolds
Theresa Sanchez-Baker

Proofreader
Kathleen Prata

Indexer
Steve Rath

Cover Design
University Graphics

Book Design
Kavish + Kavish

Contents at a Glance

Introduction

Greetings! Welcome to *Microsoft Office 4 For Windows For Dummies Quick Reference,* the Microsoft Office reference book that's less filling and looks great.

You've stumbled upon the ideal book if you use one or more of the programs that come with Microsoft Office but don't really want to become an expert in anything remotely related to computers. This Office book is for those of you who still have a life outside of Office and don't want to spend hours figuring out how to do things that should be easy.

This book does not teach you how to use Office from the ground up. If you're a complete beginner when it comes to Office, I suggest that you pick up a copy of Roger Parker's *Microsoft Office 4 For Windows For Dummies.* Or take a shopping cart through the computer book aisle at your local bookstore and get copies of *Word For Windows 6 For Dummies* (Dan Gookin), *Excel For Dummies* (Greg Harvey), *PowerPoint 4 For Windows For Dummies* (Yours Truly), and *Access 2 For Dummies* (Scott Palmer). These books are designed to teach you everything you need to know about using the programs that come with Office.

This book is meant to be more of an "I forgot how to do that" book. It's for those embarrassing moments when you should know how to insert a table of contents, but you can't quite remember which command to use. Or when you want to quickly look up the keyboard shortcut that lets you switch to outline view. Or when you know that there's a quick way to do a Word mail merge using data stored in an Access database, but you're not quite sure how to do it.

Turn to this book when you want 30-Second-Right-Now-Don't-Waste-My-Time answers to your questions. You won't find pages and pages of tireless prose exploring all the subtle nuances of each Office command. Instead, you'll get concise explanations of how to perform what I think are the most important and useful tasks and procedures. You also get easy-to-find tables of keyboard shortcuts and information about making the programs of Office work together.

How to Use This Book

Keep this book within arm's reach of your computer. Whenever you're about to do something you're not 100-percent sure about, grab this book before you reach for your mouse and look up what you're about to do to refresh your memory. Especially handy are the keyboard shortcut sections; look for the notebook-style pages in each part. You can also refresh your memory about what each basic element of the program's screen does at the beginning of each section of the book.

The best way to use this book is probably to use the index to find the procedure you're having trouble with and then turn to the indicated page to find out how to perform the procedure. Procedures that are common to all the programs — such as opening and closing files — are found in Part I. Procedures for using the various programs together are found in Part VIII. Procedures that are specific to the individual programs are found in the parts in between.

What Are All These Parts?

This book is divided into eight parts:

Part I: Welcome to Microsoft Office. This brief introduction to Microsoft Office explains what each Office program does and describes several features that are common to all the programs, like assigning filenames, opening and closing files, and so on. It also briefly explains how to use the Microsoft Office Manager program, MOM.

Part II: Word for Windows. This section contains reference information about Word for Windows, the ultimate word processing program. It presents helpful keyboard shortcuts and summarizes the steps for commonly used procedures.

Part III: Excel. This part covers Excel, the last word in spreadsheet programs. You'll find information about keyboard shortcuts and common functions and procedures.

Part IV: PowerPoint. This part covers PowerPoint, the desktop presentation program for creating slides, overhead transparencies, or on-screen slide shows. Once again, I provide information about keyboard shortcuts and procedures.

Part V: Access. If you have the Professional Edition of Microsoft Office, you'll appreciate this part, which covers the keyboard shortcuts and procedures for this top-notch database program.

Part VI: Mail. If you are a network user, Microsoft Office allows you to send or receive electronic mail by using Microsoft Mail. This part shows you how.

Part VII: Microsoft Office Applets. Microsoft Office comes with a number of smaller programs called *Applets* that you can use from within the other Office programs. These mini-programs include

Graph, Equation Editor, WordArt, OrgChart, and ClipArt Gallery. Learn how to use them in this part.

Part VIII: Working Together. This "Office is greater than the sum of its parts" section shows you how to use the various Office programs together by exchanging information between programs. For example, you'll learn how to mail merge with Excel or Access data, create a presentation from a Word outline, and analyze Access data in Excel.

What All the Pretty Pictures Mean

Just before this book went to the printer, I pelted it with a semiautomatic icon assault riffle, now illegal in 17 states. As a result, this book is strewn with little pictures designed to convey information quickly. Here's the lowdown on the icons you'll find:

This procedure is a no-brainer — so simple that even an adult can do it.

This procedure is a bit tricky. It isn't rocket science, but you should pay attention when using it to avoid potentially damaging mistakes.

Clear your desk before attempting this operation. It requires your full attention from start to finish.

You can use this procedure to exchange information between the various Office programs.

This procedure is similar (maybe even identical) to those found in other Office programs.

Danger! Danger! You may be putting your files, your system, or yourself at risk if you don't heed these warnings.

This little tidbit of helpful information can save you time and effort.

This icon indicates that you can find more information about a particular topic elsewhere within this book.

This icon indicates that you can find more information about a particular topic in *Microsoft Office 4 For Windows For Dummies* or one of the other *...For Dummies* books.

Part 1

Welcome to Microsoft Office

This part describes the uses of the various programs that make up Office and describes certain features that work pretty much the same in all the programs, such as using the mouse and keyboard, getting help, and other enlightening tidbits.

What Do All Those Programs Do?

The standard Microsoft Office package comes with four programs: Word, Excel, PowerPoint, and Mail. The more expensive Microsoft Office Professional comes with the same four programs plus a program called Access. In addition, both packages come with a handy little program called Microsoft Office Manager.

Hi MOM!

Microsoft Office Manager (lovingly known as *MOM*) is a little program that bunches all the Office programs together in a handy toolbar so you can easily launch or switch between the programs. When you install Office, MOM is inserted into your Startup program group so that it is available at all times.

The following table summarizes some of the more interesting things you can do with MOM.

Action	What It Does
Click a button	Starts the indicated program. If the program is already running, switches to the program.
Ctrl+click a button	Starts a new instance of the indicated program, even if the program is already running.

(continued)

Action	What It Does
Shift+click a button	Starts or switches to the indicated program and arranges the windows so that both the program you are using when you click the button and the program you start or switch to are visible at the same time. (This process is hard to describe, but try it once and you'll see what I mean.)
Alt+click a button	Exits the indicated program.
Click the Office button	Activates the MOM menu. This menu includes commands to run the Office programs or Windows' own Program Manager or File Manager. The menu also lets you configure MOM's appearance and operation.

⚟⚟⚟⚟⚟⚟ ———— The MOM toolbar

Word for Windows

Word for Windows, usually called just *Word* and sometimes *WinWord,* is one of the best word processing programs available. It lets you create documents of all shapes and sizes, from small letters and memos to medium-sized term papers and reports to humongous books and health care reform proposals. Office comes with Version 6 of Word.

Word's features let you add drawings and graphs to your documents, create perfectly aligned tables, spew forth junk mail to your friends and enemies, and who knows what else. Although Word is not a full-fledged desktop publishing program, it is suitable for many desktop publishing tasks, such as producing simple brochures and newsletters.

See Part II of this book for more information about Word.

For detailed information about Word, see *Word For Windows 6 For Dummies, MORE Word For Windows 6 For Dummies,* and Chapters 1 – 4 of *Microsoft Office 4 For Windows For Dummies.*

Excel

Excel, a spreadsheet program, is the brains of the Office operation. Excel excels at adding up budget totals, calculating sales commissions, figuring loan payments, and performing other math-oriented chores. Office comes with Version 5 of Excel.

Like other spreadsheet programs, Excel presents data as a large table that consists of rows and columns. The intersection of a row and column is called a *cell*. You can use cells to store text, numbers, or formulas that calculate results based on the contents of other cells.

 You can find reference information for Excel in Part III of this book.

 For complete information, check out *Excel For Dummies,* Second Edition, *MORE Excel 5 For Dummies,* and Chapters 5 – 7 of *Microsoft Office 4 For Windows For Dummies.*

PowerPoint

PowerPoint is the oddball program of the Office suite. Many people buy Office because they need a word processor and a spreadsheet program, and it's cheaper to buy the basic Office package than it is to buy Word and Excel separately. So the rest of what comes with Office (read: PowerPoint) is basically free. Office 4 comes with Version 4 of PowerPoint.

So what the heck is PowerPoint? It's a *desktop presentation program*, which means that it's designed to help you make presentations. You can use it whether you're speaking in front of hundreds of people at a shareholders' meeting, to a group of sales reps at a sales conference, or one-on-one with a client at a restaurant.

If you work with overhead transparencies or 35mm slides, PowerPoint is just the program you need. PowerPoint can create slides in any of several formats; in addition, it can create hand-outs for your audience and notes for you so that you don't get lost in the middle of your speech.

 Check out Part IV of this book for reference information about PowerPoint.

 For details about using PowerPoint, see *PowerPoint 4 For Windows For Dummies* or Chapters 8 and 9 of *Microsoft Office 4 For Windows For Dummies.*

Access

Access, a database program, is the computer equivalent of the shoe box in which you store your tax records. The difference between Access and a shoe box is that Access keeps your records in order, lets you print reports that list and summarize your data in any form imaginable, and doesn't crumple your papers. Office comes with Access Version 2.

Access is included only in the more expensive Professional edition of Microsoft Office; it doesn't come with the bargain-basement Standard edition.

Of the programs that come with Office, Access is the hardest one to learn. Database programs such as Access are well suited for keeping mailing lists, but if a mailing list is the only reason you need Access, don't bother. Word does a pretty good job of storing mailing lists all by itself.

See Part V of this book for more information about Access.

Check out *Access 2 For Dummies* or Chapters 10 and 11 of *Microsoft Office 4 For Windows For Dummies* for the complete lowdown on Access.

Mail

Mail is an electronic-mail program that lets you exchange messages with other computer users when your computer is connected to a network. It is your portal to the infamous Information Superhighway.

It's a little misleading to say that Office comes with Mail. Office doesn't include program diskettes that let you install Mail. Instead, it comes with a piece of paper that says that you can legally use Mail on your computer. But before you can do that, the pocket protector-clad gurus who run your computer's network must first install a separately purchased Microsoft Mail program on the network. If your network doesn't already have Microsoft Mail, you're out of luck.

See Part VI of this book for more information about Mail.

Chapter 12 of *Microsoft Office 4 For Windows For Dummies* spells out the details of using Mail.

Those little Applet programs

In addition to the programs I just described, Office comes with a number of smaller programs that are designed to be used from within the other programs. These smaller programs are often called *Applets* and include Graph, WordArt, OrgChart, Equation Editor, and Clip Art Gallery.

Reference information for the Applet programs is located in Part VII of this book.

Graph

Graph is the charting module that comes with Office. It's suitable for creating bar, line, and pie charts and a bevy of other chart types that come in handy from time to time. You can access Graph from Word, Excel, PowerPoint, or Access.

WordArt

WordArt is a graphics program designed to create logos and other fancy text effects. You can use it to stretch text so that it disappears into the horizon or follows a curve, add a three-dimensional look to text, or otherwise embellish your text. It's used mostly with Word and PowerPoint.

OrgChart

OrgChart is designed to create organizational charts that show who reports to whom and where the buck stops. OrgChart is used mostly from PowerPoint, but you can access it from the other programs as well.

Equation Editor

Move over, Einstein! Office comes with an equation editor called — hold on to your hat — Microsoft Equation Editor, which can help you draw simple equations like e=mc^2 or complex equations such as this one:

$$\mu_{Y.X} = \overline{Y}_X \pm t_\alpha s_{Y.X} \sqrt{\frac{1}{n} + \frac{(X - \overline{X})^2}{\sum X^2 - n\overline{X}^2}}$$

Equation Editor is actually a special version of a gee-whiz math program called MathType, created by Design Science.

ClipArt Gallery

ClipArt Gallery is a centralized storehouse for clip art that eliminates the need to rifle through various directories trying to find just the right bit of clip art based on an esoteric DOS filename. With ClipArt Gallery, you can actually *see* your clip art before you copy it into your document.

Using Your Mouse

Remember that scene in *Star Trek IV* in which Scotty, zapped back into the 1980s and forced to use a primitive computer (it was a Macintosh), picks up the mouse and talks into it like a microphone? "Computer! Hello, computer? Hmmph. How quaint."

You won't get very far with any of the programs that come with Office until you learn how to use the mouse. You can try picking it up and talking into it if you want, but you won't get any better results than Scotty did.

A few mouse tricks work similarly in all the programs that come with Office, as the following table describes.

Mouse Action	*Explanation*
Double-click text	Selects a whole word.
Ctrl+click text	Selects an entire sentence.
Triple-click text	Selects a whole paragraph.
Right-click anywhere	Calls up a shortcut menu.
Shift+drag	Hold down the Shift key when drawing shapes to force lines to be horizontal or vertical, force arcs and ellipses to be true circles, or force rectangles to be squares.
Ctrl+drag	Hold down the Ctrl key when drawing shapes to draw from the center rather than from end to end.
Ctrl+Shift+drag	Hold down the Ctrl and Shift keys while drawing shapes to draw from the center and to enforce squareness.

Working Smart with the Keyboard

If you're the type who never likes to move your fingers from home position, you'll be relieved to know that the programs that come with Office are rife with keyboard shortcuts. To make keyboard life easier, the keyboard shortcuts for those functions found in all (or at least most) of the Office programs are the same. The following listings summarize those functions.

Editing Commands

Keyboard Shortcut	*Equivalent Command*
Ctrl+X	Edit⇨Cut
Ctrl+C	Edit⇨Copy
Ctrl+V	Edit⇨Paste
Ctrl+Z	Edit⇨Undo
Ctrl+Y	Edit⇨Redo
Ctrl+A	Edit⇨Select All
Ctrl+F	Edit⇨Find
Ctrl+H	Edit⇨Replace

File Commands

Keyboard Shortcut	*Equivalent Command*
Ctrl+N	File⇨New
Ctrl+O	File⇨Open
Ctrl+S	File⇨Save
F12	File⇨Save As
Ctrl+W	File⇨Close
Ctrl+P	File⇨Print
Ctrl+F12	File⇨Print Preview
Alt+F4	File⇨Exit

Quick Formatting

Keyboard Shortcut	*Equivalent Command*
Ctrl+B	Bold
Ctrl+I	Italic
Ctrl+U	Underline
Ctrl+spacebar	Return to normal format

Switching Programs

Keyboard Shortcut	*What It Does*
Alt+Esc	Switches to the next program in line.
Alt+Tab	Displays the name of the next program in line. While holding down the Alt key, keep pressing Tab until the name of the program you want appears. Release both keys to switch to that program.
Ctrl+Esc	Pops up a list of all active programs. Double-click the one you want to switch to.

Naming Files

DOS is very strict about the names it lets you use for files. Obey the following restrictions and you will be a happy user all the days of your life:

- No more than 8 characters per filename, please.

- You can use letters and numbers. Avoid special characters like #, $, and %; some of them are allowed, but others aren't. I never can remember which are which, so I just avoid them all.

- DOS lets you add a three-character *extension* to the end of the filename. The extension is separated from the rest of the filename by a period. The period isn't part of the filename itself; it's just a separator. The following table lists the extensions used by Office programs.

Program	Extension	Usage
Word	DOC	Document file
	DOT	Template file
Excel	XLS	Workbook file
	XLT	Template file
PowerPoint	PPT	Presentation file
Access	MDB	Database file

Here are some allowable filenames for various types of files:

SALES.XLS — A perfectly acceptable filename, although it's pretty generic. If you create only one sales spreadsheet in your lifetime, it will suffice. Otherwise, a more specific filename is in order.

BRODART.XLS — Ah, now this one is better. Here, the filename indicates the client tracked by the spreadsheet. But you're still stuck if you need to keep more than one spreadsheet for this client.

BROD001.XLS — Even better. See how you can freely mix letters and numbers?

27.DOC — No problem. You can use numbers by themselves.

3BQ4-72C.PPT — Still not a problem. The hyphen is one of those allowable special characters. The only problem with this filename is that you have to work for a government procurement office to know what it stands for.

Here are some filenames that won't work:

MY CLASS.PPT	Nope. No spaces allowed in the middle of filenames.
34+35.MDB	Nope. The hyphen or minus sign is OK, but the plus sign isn't. Best to avoid them all.
ECONOMICS.DOC	Nope. Too many letters. Sorry.
TRY.THIS.ONE	Nope. Too many periods.
$@#&!.*#!	Nope. Profane filename. Makes DOS blush.

Getting Help

Lost within the dark woods of Office and don't know how to get out? Fret not, for all the Office programs boast an excellent help system that can answer all your questions — provided, of course, that you know what your questions are.

Although the type of help available varies from program to program, the details of how to wade your way through the volumes of help information is the same for all the Office programs. The following list summarizes the more notable methods of getting help.

- When lost at sea, the universal help signal is S.O.S. When lost in Office, the universal help signal is F1. Press F1 at any time and help is on its way.

- If you press F1 when you're in the middle of something, odds are that you'll be shown help on doing only the task you were trying to accomplish. This slick little bit of wizardry is called *context-sensitive help.*

- When you click Help in the menu bar, you get a whole menu of help stuff, most of which is only moderately helpful. Help⇨Contents shows a list of broad help categories from which you can pick. It's a useful command when you're not sure what you're looking for. Help⇨Index gives you an A-to-Z index of all help topics. And Help⇨Search lets you search the index by typing a portion of the word you want to look up.

- You can also call up help on just about any dialog box by clicking the Help button that appears in the box.

- You can also use the Help tool in the Standard toolbar. Frankly, it's a little weird. Click it, and the cursor becomes an arrow with a question mark grafted onto its back. Point it at just about anything on-screen and click to get help about the thing you point at.

Best Loved Procedures

Although the programs that come with Office have many differences, they also have many things in common. The sections that follow describe several commonly used procedures that work pretty much the same no matter which Office program you're using.

Starting a Program

To start an Office program, follow these steps:

1. Light some votive candles and sit in the Lotus position facing Redmond, Washington.

2. Start your computer. Hopefully, you have to flip only one switch to do so. But if your computer, monitor, and printer are plugged in separately, you have to turn on each one separately.

3. If Windows doesn't start up all by itself, start Windows by typing **WIN** at the DOS prompt.

4. Find the Microsoft Office program group. If it isn't already open, double-click the Microsoft Office icon to open the group.

5. Double-click the icon for the program you want to start.

A faster way to start an Office program is to locate the MOM toolbar and click the button for the program you want to start. (The MOM toolbar appears if the Microsoft Office Manager program is located in your Startup group.)

Exiting a Program

Had enough excitement for one day? Use any one of these techniques to shut down your program:

- Choose File⇨Exit.

- Double-click the control box at the upper-left corner of the program window.

- Press Alt+F4.

You aren't allowed to abandon ship until you save your work. If you've made changes to any presentation files and haven't saved them, a dialog box asks whether you want to save your files.

Never, never, never, never, never, *ever* just turn off your computer while a program is running. You may as well pour acid into the keyboard or run over the motherboard with a truck. *Always* exit all programs that are running before you turn off your computer.

In fact, you'd best get clean out of Windows before shutting down your computer. After you exit all your programs and all that's left is Windows, exit it by using one of the preceding methods. Only when you see the happy DOS prompt (C>) can you safely turn off your computer.

Saving a File

After you finish your document, spreadsheet, or presentation, you can print it and turn off your computer, right? Wrong! All your precious work is held in your computer's fleeting RAM memory until you save your work to a disk file. Turn off your computer before you save your work, and — poof! — your work vanishes as though David Copperfield were in town.

You can save a file to disk in four ways:

- Click the Save button in the Standard toolbar.
- Choose File⇨Save.
- Press Ctrl+S.
- Press Shift+F12.

If you haven't yet saved the file to disk, the magical Save As dialog box appears, in which you can type the name you want to use for the file:

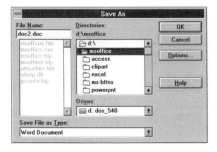

Type a filename for your file and then click the OK button to save the file. After you save the file, subsequent saves update the disk file with any changes you made to the file since you saved it last.

Use your head when assigning a name to a new file. The filename will help you recognize the file later on, so pick a meaningful name that suggests the file's contents.

After you save a file for the first time, the name of the file in the window's title bar changes to indicate the name of the file. If you ever forget which file you're working on, just check the title bar.

Don't work on your file for hours at a time without saving it. I've learned the hard way to save my work often. Get into the habit of pressing Ctrl+S every few minutes, especially after making a significant change to a file.

Saving a File under a New Name

If you want to make a duplicate of the current file using a different filename, follow these steps:

1. Call up the File➪Save As command. The Save As dialog box appears (see the preceding section).

2. Use the Drives and Directories controls to rummage about until you find the drive and directory in which you want to save the file.

3. Type a new name for the file in the File Name text box.

4. Click OK.

Retrieving an Existing File

Having saved your file to disk, you'll probably want to retrieve it later to make additional changes or print it. There are at least four ways to do so:

- Click the Open button in the Standard toolbar.
- Choose File➪Open.
- Press Ctrl+O.
- Press Ctrl+F12.

All four commands pop up the Open dialog box, which gives you a list of files to choose from:

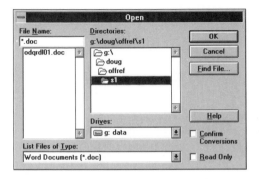

Click the file you want and then click the OK button or press the Enter key. The file is read from disk into your computer's RAM. If the file isn't immediately visible, use the Dri̲ves and D̲irectories lists to rummage about your disk until you find the file.

The fastest way to open a file from the Open dialog box is to double-click the file you want to open. Doing so spares you from having to click once on the file and then a second time on the OK button. It also exercises the fast-twitch muscles in your index finger.

All the Office programs keep track of the last few files you've opened and display them right in the File menu. To reopen a file you've opened recently, click the F̲ile menu and inspect the list of files at the bottom of the menu. If the file you want is in the list, click it to open it.

Printing a File

Follow this procedure to print your masterpiece:

1. Make sure that your printer is turned on and ready to print.

 2. Click the Print button in the Standard toolbar.

3. When the Print dialog box appears, peruse its options. Most Office programs let you indicate whether you want to print the entire file or just specific pages, and some have other interesting print options as well. The following figure shows what Word's Print dialog box looks like (the Print dialog box in the other Office programs is similar).

4. Click OK.

Printed pages should soon appear on your printer. Check them to make sure that they look the way you want.

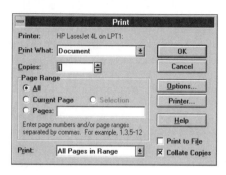

As with many other Office functions, you can invoke the printing functions in at least four ways:

- Call up the File⇨Print command.
- Click the Print button.
- Press Ctrl+P.
- Press Ctrl+Shift+F12.

Closing a File

Closing a file is kind of like gathering up your papers, putting them neatly in a file folder, and returning the folder to its proper file drawer. The file disappears from your computer screen, but don't worry: it's tucked safely away on your hard disk, where you can get to it later if you need to.

To close a file, choose File⇨Close. You can also use the keyboard shortcut Ctrl+W, but you'd have to have a mind like a steel trap to remember that Ctrl+W stands for Close.

You don't have to close files before exiting the program. If you exit the program without closing a file, it closes the file for you. The only occasion when you may want to close a file is when you want to work on a different file and don't want to keep both files open at the same time.

If you've made changes since the last time you saved the file, a dialog box appears, offering to save the changes for you. Click Yes to save the file before closing, or click No to abandon any changes you made to the file.

If you have only one file open and you close it, you may discover that most of the program's commands are rendered useless. Fear not. Open another file or create a new file, and the commands return to life.

Part II

Word for Windows

 This part covers the word processor of word processors, Microsoft Word for Windows 6. It's impossible to cover everything that you can do with Word in a few pages, so this part out of necessity covers just the basics. You'll find lots more information in *Word For Windows 6 For Dummies* and *MORE Word For Windows 6 For Dummies*.

The Word Screen

The following figure shows what Word's screen looks like when you're editing a document.

In the center of the screen is the main document window. In this example, only one document is open and its window is maximized so that it fills all the space available within the main Word window. However, you can open more than one document and display them in separately sizable document windows.

The status bar provides helpful information about the document. The scroll bars along the right and bottom edges of the screen allow you to navigate though your document. In addition, the horizontal scroll bar's three view buttons let you switch among the three basic document views.

You can call up a special control menu by clicking the application control box, or you can quickly quit Word by double-clicking it. You can also use the Minimize and Maximize buttons to alter the size of Word's window.

The control box at the left edge of the menu bar and the Restore button at the right edge of the menu bar are for the current document window, which is maximized so that it fills all the available space within the main Word window. If the document window isn't maximized, these buttons appear in the title bar of the document window rather than in the menu bar.

Formatting toolbar
Standard toolbar
Control box
Vertical scroll bar
Restore button

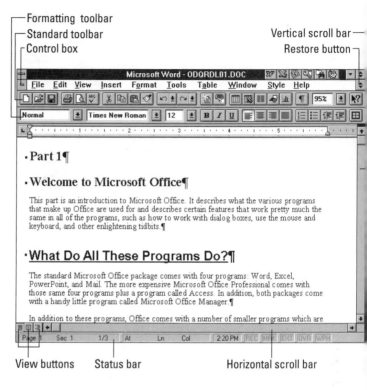

View buttons   Status bar   Horizontal scroll bar

The Standard toolbar contains a variety of buttons that perform frequently used functions. Just click a button to perform the function. To find out what each button does, hold the mouse over the button for a moment. A bright yellow tool tip appears, indicating the button's function. The Formatting toolbar, immediately below, lets you quickly apply the most common formats, including style, font, size, bold, italic, underline, alignment, numbered and bulleted lists, and indentation.

Roll Call of Keyboard Shortcuts

Nothing is more irritating than flying along in Word at 75 words per minute only to have to reach for the mouse to click a button or menu. The good news is that you can do almost everything that can be done in Word with keyboard shortcuts that rarely force you to leave home position. The bad news is that you'll never manage to commit all these shortcuts to memory; there are just too many of them. With practice, though, you should have little trouble learning the keyboard shortcuts for the Word commands you use most.

If some of the following keyboard shortcuts don't work for you, don't panic. The likely cause is that you or someone else has used the Tools⇨Customize command to change the default keyboard shortcuts. Keyboard customizations are stored as a part of the document template, so you may find that a shortcut works sometimes and doesn't work at other times, depending on which template is attached to the document.

You can quickly restore all Word keyboard shortcuts to their default settings by calling up the Tools⇨Customize command, clicking the Keyboard tab, and then clicking the Reset All button. When a confirmation dialog box appears, click the Yes button and then click the Close button.

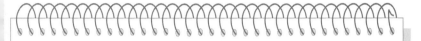

Character Formatting

Shortcut	What It Does
Ctrl+B	Makes text **bold**.
Ctrl+I	Sets the font to *italic.*
Ctrl+U	Underlines text (continuous).
Ctrl+Shift+W	Underlines words.
Ctrl+Shift+D	Double underlines text.
Ctrl+Shift+A	Sets the font to ALL CAPS.
Ctrl+Shift+K	Sets the font to SMALL CAPS.
Ctrl+=	Uses $_{subscript}$ font.
Ctrl+Shift+=	Uses ^{superscript} font.
Ctrl+Shift+H	Makes the text hidden.
Shift+F3	Changes case.
Ctrl+Shift+*	Displays nonprinting characters.
Ctrl+Shift+F	Changes font.
Ctrl+Shift+P	Changes point size.
Ctrl+]	Increases size by one point.
Ctrl+[	Decreases size by one point.

(continued)

Shortcut	What It Does
Ctrl+Shift+>	Increases size to next available size.
Ctrl+Shift+<	Decreases size to preceding available size.
Ctrl+Shift+Q	Switches to Symbol font (Γρεεκ Τραγεδψ).
Ctrl+Shift+Z	Removes character formatting.
Ctrl+spacebar	Removes character formatting.

Editing

Shortcut	What It Does
Ctrl+X	Cuts text to the Clipboard.
Ctrl+C	Copies text to the Clipboard.
Ctrl+V	Pastes text from the Clipboard.
Ctrl+Z	Undoes the most recent command.
Ctrl+Y	Redoes an undone command.
Ctrl+F3	Cuts to the spike.
Ctrl+Shift+F3	Pastes the contents of the spike.
Ctrl+Del	Deletes a word (forward).
Ctrl+Backspace	Deletes a word (backward).
Ctrl+F	Finds text.
Ctrl+H	Replaces occurrences of one text string with another.
Ctrl+A	Selects the entire document.

Fields

Shortcut	What It Does
F9	Updates the selected field or fields.
Shift+F9	Switches the display between field codes and field results for the selected field or fields.
Alt+F9	Switches the display between field codes and field results for all fields in the document.
Ctrl+F9	Inserts a field into a document.

(continued)

Shortcut	What It Does
Ctrl+Shift+F9	Converts a field to a text value.
F11	Finds the next field in the document.
Shift+F11	Finds the preceding field in the document.
Ctrl+F11	Locks a field so it cannot be updated.
Ctrl+Shift+F11	Unlocks a field.
Alt+Shift+D	Inserts a DATE field.
Alt+Shift+P	Inserts a PAGE field.
Alt+Shift+T	Inserts a TIME field.

File Management

Shortcut	What It Does
Ctrl+N	Creates a new file.
Ctrl+O	Opens an existing file.
Ctrl+W	Closes the file.
Ctrl+S	Saves the file.
F12	Saves the file using a new filename.
Ctrl+P	Prints a file.
Ctrl+F2	Accesses Print Preview.
Alt+F4	Exits the application.
Ctrl+F6	Moves to the next document window.
Ctrl+Shift+F6	Goes back to the preceding document window.

Navigating and Selecting

Shortcut	What It Does
Ctrl+←	Moves one word left.
Ctrl+→	Moves one word right.
Ctrl+↑	Goes back to the preceding paragraph.
Ctrl+↓	Goes to the next paragraph.
End	Goes to end of the line.
Home	Goes to beginning of the line.

(continued)

Shortcut	What It Does
PgUp	Goes back to the preceding screen.
PgDn	Goes on to the next screen.
Ctrl+PgUp	Takes you to the top of the screen.
Ctrl+PgDn	Takes you to the bottom of the screen.
Ctrl+Alt+PgUp	Takes you to the preceding page.
Ctrl+Alt+PgDn	Takes you to the next page.
Ctrl+End	Takes you to the end of the document.
Ctrl+Home	Takes you to the beginning of the document.
Ctrl+G	Goes to the page you specify.

TIP You can select text by holding down the Shift key while using these keyboard shortcuts (except Ctrl+G). For example, to select several words, move the insertion point to the beginning of the first word you want to select. Then hold down the Shift key and press Ctrl+→ for each word you want to select.

Paragraph Formatting

Shortcut	What It Does
Ctrl+L	Left-aligns a paragraph.
Ctrl+R	Right-aligns a paragraph.
Ctrl+J	Justifies a paragraph.
Ctrl+E	Centers a paragraph.
Ctrl+M	Increases left indent.
Ctrl+Shift+M	Reduces left indent.
Ctrl+T	Creates a hanging indent.
Ctrl+Shift+T	Reduces a hanging indent.
Ctrl+1	Single-spaces a paragraph.
Ctrl+2	Double-spaces a paragraph.
Ctrl+5	Sets line spacing to 1.5.
Ctrl+0 (zero)	Removes or sets space before to one line.
Ctrl+Shift+S	Applies a style.
Ctrl+K	AutoFormats.
Ctrl+Shift+N	Applies Normal style.

(continued)

Shortcut	*What It Does*
Ctrl+Alt+1	Applies Heading 1 style.
Ctrl+Alt+2	Applies Heading 2 style.
Ctrl+Alt+3	Applies Heading 3 style.
Ctrl+Shift+L	Applies List style.
Ctrl+Q	Removes paragraph formatting.

Outlines

Shortcut	*What It Does*
Ctrl+Alt+O	Switches to outline view.
Ctrl+Alt+N	Switches back to normal view.
Alt+Shift+A	Collapses or expands all text.
Alt+Shift+− (on numeric keypad)	Collapses the selection.
Alt+Shift++ (on numeric keypad)	Expands the selection.
Alt+Shift+1	Collapses/expands to heading level 1.
Alt+Shift+(number)	Collapses/expands to specified heading level.
/ (on numeric keypad)	Hides/shows formatting.
Shift+Tab	Promotes the selection.
Alt+Shift+←	Promotes the selection.
Tab	Demotes the selection.
Alt+Shift+→	Demotes the selection.
Ctrl+Shift+N	Demotes to body text by applying Normal style.
Alt+Shift+↑	Moves the selection up one paragraph at a time.
Alt+Shift+↓	Moves the selection down one paragraph at a time.

Special Characters

Shortcut	*Character It Inserts*
Ctrl+-(hyphen)	Optional hyphen
Ctrl+Shift+-(hyphen)	Nonbreaking hyphen

(continued)

Ctrl+Shift+spacebar	Nonbreaking space
Ctrl+Alt+C	Copyright symbol (©)
Ctrl+Alt+R	Registered trademark symbol (®)
Ctrl+Alt+. (period)	Ellipsis (…)
Ctrl+', '	Single open quote (')
Ctrl+', '	Single close quote (')
Ctrl+', "	Double open quote (")
Ctrl+', "	Double close quote (")
Ctrl+– (on numeric keypad)	En dash (–)
Ctrl+Alt+– (on numeric keypad)	Em dash (—)

Views

Shortcut	What It Does
Ctrl+Alt+N	Switches to normal view.
Ctrl+Alt+O	Switches to outline view.
Ctrl+Alt+P	Switches to page layout view.

Best Loved Procedures

The following sections contain a hodge-podge of procedures for working with various aspects of Word.

Borders: Adding Borders to a Paragraph

To add a border around a text paragraph, follow these steps:

1. Select the paragraph to which you want to add a border.

2. Choose the Format⇨Borders and Shading command to access the following dialog box.

3. Click the Box icon to wrap a border all the way around the paragraph.

4. Select a line style from the Style list if you don't like the default style.

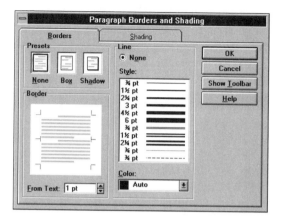

5. If you want less than a full box all the way around the paragraph, click those portions of the border you don't want in the Bo_r_der preview area. For example, to place a line only underneath the paragraph, click the left, right, and top lines to eliminate them.

6. Click OK when you're done.

You can specify a different style for each border line. The borders created when you click the Sh_a_dow icon instead of the Bo_x_ icon have thicker lines for the right and bottom lines to create a shadowed look.

To get rid of a border, choose F_o_rmat⇨_B_orders and Shading and select _N_one for the border type.

 You can also apply borders by clicking the Borders button and then using the various buttons that appear on the Borders toolbar.

 For more information, see Chapter 22 in *Word For Windows 6 For Dummies.*

Columns: Setting the Column Layout

Here's how to create multiple columns in your document:

 1. Click the Columns button in the Standard toolbar to bring up the drop-down menu shown here.

2. Drag the mouse to pick the number of columns you want.

3. Let go.

Voilà! The document is formatted with the number of columns you select.

In normal view (View⇨Normal), the text is formatted according to the width of the column, but the columns are not displayed on-screen side by side. To see both columns side by side on-screen, switch to Page Layout view by choosing View⇨Page Layout.

For a quick glimpse of how the columns appear when printed, choose the File⇨Print Preview command. When you've seen enough, click the Close button to return to your document.

The Columns button lets you set the number of columns, but it doesn't let you control the size of each column or the amount of space between columns. To do so, call up the Format⇨Columns command and play with its settings.

For more information, see Chapter 12 in *Word For Windows 6 For Dummies* or Chapter 10 in *MORE Word For Windows 6 For Dummies*.

Envelopes: Printing an Envelope

Word's Tools⇨Envelopes and Labels command makes it easy to print envelopes. Here's the blow-by-blow procedure:

1. If you're printing an envelope to mail a letter in, create and print the letter first. Doing so saves you the trouble of typing the mailing address twice.

2. Call up the Tools⇨Envelopes and Labels command. The Envelopes and Labels dialog box appears:

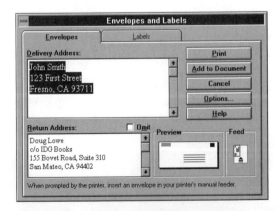

3. Check the address in the Delivery Address field. Word can usually ferret out the mailing address from an ordinary letter. If not, you have to enter the address yourself.

4. Insert an envelope into your printer.

5. Click the Print button. That's all!

Find: Finding Missing Text

You can use the Edit⇨Find command to find text anywhere in a document. Just follow these steps:

1. Choose Edit⇨Find or press Ctrl+F to summon the Find dialog box.

2. Type the text you want to find in the Find What field.

3. Click the Find Next button.

4. Wait a second while Word searches your document. When it finds the text, it highlights it on-screen. The Find dialog box remains on-screen so you can click Find Next to find yet another occurrence of the text.

5. When it can find no more occurrences of the text, Word displays the following message:

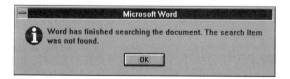

Click OK and get on with your life.

You can bail out of the Find dialog box by clicking Cancel or pressing Esc.

You can change the direction of Word's search by changing the setting in the Search drop-down box. Three choices are available:

- **Down:** Starts the search at the position of the insertion point and searches forward toward the end of the document.

- **Up:** Searches backward from the insertion point toward the beginning of the document.

- **All:** Searches the entire document without regard to the position of the insertion point.

Check the Match Case option before beginning the search if it matters whether the text appears in uppercase or lowercase letters. This option is handy when you have, for example, a document about Mr. Smith the blacksmith.

Speaking of Mr. Smith the blacksmith, use the Match Whole Word Only option to find your text only when it appears as a whole word. If you want to find the text where you talk about Mr. Smith the blacksmith's mit, for example, type **mit** in the Find What text and check the Match Whole Word Only option. That way, the Find command looks for *mit* as a separate word. It doesn't show you all the *mit*s in Smith and Blacksmith.

Check the Use Pattern Matching option if you want to include wildcard characters in the Find What field. Here are three of the most useful wildcards:

- **?** finds a single occurrence of any character. For example, **f?t** finds *fat* or *fit*.

- ***** finds any combination of characters. For example, **b*t** finds any combination of characters that begins with *b* and ends with *t*, such as *bat*, *bait*, *ballast*, or *bacteriologist*.

- **[abc]** finds any one of the characters enclosed in the brackets. For example, **b[ai]t** finds *bat* or *bit* but not *bet* or *but*.

Check the Sounds Like option if you're not sure exactly how to spell the text you're looking for.

If you find the text you're looking for and decide that you want to replace it with something else, click the Replace button. Then skip ahead to "Replace: Replacing Text."

Find: Finding Style Formatting

Here's the procedure for finding paragraphs tagged with a particular style:

1. Invoke the Edit⇨Find command. The keyboard shortcut is Ctrl+F. Either way, the Find dialog box appears.

2. Click the Format button and then choose the Style command from the pop-up menu. The Find Style dialog box appears, as shown in the next figure.

3. In the Find Style dialog box, scroll through the list of styles until you locate the one you want to find. Click it and then click OK.

Notice how the style is indicated in the Format box, just below the Find What field:

Make sure that the Find What field itself is blank; otherwise, the Find command searches for specific text that's formatted with the style you specify.

4. Click the Find Next button to find the next occurrence of the style. Click it again to find the next occurrence. It's like déjà vu all over again.

5. Press Esc after you're done.

You can also replace paragraph styles by following a similar procedure involving the Edit⇨Replace command. Click in the Find What field and then use the Format button to choose the style you want to find and replace. Then click in the Replace With field and use the Format button to choose the style with which you want to replace the Find What style. Finally, use the Find Next and Replace buttons to find and replace the paragraph styles.

Footnotes: Adding a Footnote

Follow this procedure to add footnotes to your documents:

1. Put the cursor where you want the little footnote reference number to appear in your text.

2. Choose the Insert⇔Footnote command to summon this dialog box:

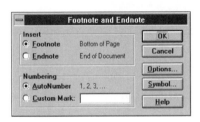

3. Click OK.

Doing so opens a separate footnote window at the bottom of the screen, where you can type your footnote.

4. Click Close after you're done.

Word automatically numbers footnotes for you. When you use the Insert⇔Footnote command, Word inserts the little footnote reference number in the text and pairs it with a number in the footnote itself. If you go back later and insert a new footnote prior to an existing one, Word automatically juggles the footnote numbers to keep everything in sync.

For an extra-quick way to create a footnote, press Ctrl+Alt+F.

To look at your footnotes, use the View⇔Footnotes command.

If you made a goof in the footnote, double-click the footnote reference in the text. Then use the footnote window to fix the note.

To delete a footnote, select its footnote reference in the text and press Delete.

For more information, see Chapter 11 in *Word For Windows 6 For Dummies* or Chapter 7 in *MORE Word For Windows 6 For Dummies*.

Formatting: Setting the Character Format

You can set character formats by using the formatting keyboard shortcuts listed earlier in this part. Or you can use the following procedure to apply character formats via the Format⇔Font command:

1. Highlight the text to which you want to apply the formatting. (If you skip this step, formatting is applied to all new text you type until you repeat the procedure to deactivate the formatting.)

2. Call up the F<u>o</u>rmat⇨<u>F</u>ont command. The Font dialog box appears:

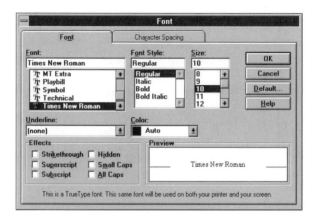

3. Play with the controls to set the <u>F</u>ont, the F<u>o</u>nt Style (bold, italic, and so on), and the <u>S</u>ize. Click the Effects you want (Stri<u>k</u>ethrough, Su<u>p</u>erscript, and so on). Use the drop-down list boxes to set the <u>U</u>nderline and <u>C</u>olor.

4. Click OK when you've had enough.

Formatting: Setting the Paragraph Format

You can set paragraph formats by using the formatting keyboard shortcuts listed earlier in this part. Or you can use the following procedure to apply paragraph formats via the F<u>o</u>rmat⇨<u>P</u>aragraph command:

1. Click anywhere in the paragraph you want to format.

2. Call up the F<u>o</u>rmat⇨<u>P</u>aragraph command. The Paragraph dialog box appears:

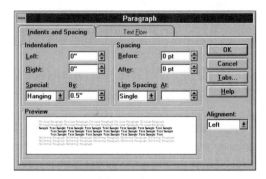

3. Play with the controls to set the Left or Right indentation or set a First Line or Hanging indent from the Special drop-down list box. You can also increase or decrease the amount of spacing Before and After the paragraph and set the Line Spacing. Notice also the Alignment drop-down list box hiding in the corner, which lets you set Left, Centered, Right, or Justified alignment.

4. Click OK after you've had enough.

Headers and Footers: Adding a Header or Footer

To add a header or footer to a document, follow these steps:

1. Call up the View⇨Header and Footer command. The Header and Footer toolbar appears along with the header of the current page.

2. If you want to add a footer, click the Switch Between Header and Footer button.

3. Type your header or footer text, formatting it any way you want.

4. Click the other buttons in the Header and Footer toolbar to add the page number, date, or time.

5. Click Close when you're done.

For more information, see Chapter 11 in *Word For Windows 6 For Dummies*.

Keyboard: Creating a Keyboard Shortcut

As if Word didn't already have enough keyboard shortcuts, it lets you easily create your own. You can assign your own keyboard shortcuts to styles, macros, fonts, AutoText entries, commands, and symbols. Just follow these steps:

1. Call up the Tools⇨Customize command to pop up the Customize dialog box. Make sure that the Keyboard tab is the frontmost tab.

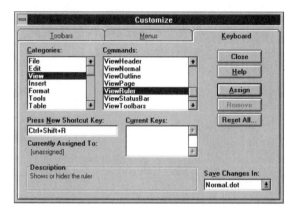

2. Select the command, style, macro, font, or other item for which you want to create a keyboard shortcut by using the Categories and Commands lists.

3. Click in the Press New Shortcut Key field and then type the new keyboard shortcut.

4. Click Assign to assign the keyboard shortcut. Then click Close.

You can also assign keyboard shortcuts by clicking the Shortcut Key from the Insert Symbol command or the Format⇨Style⇨ Modify command.

 To reset all keyboard shortcuts to their Word defaults, call up the Tools⇨Customize command, select the Keyboard tab, and click the Reset All button.

For more information, see Chapter 15 in *MORE Word For Windows 6 For Dummies.*

Lists: Creating a Bulleted List

To create a bulleted list, follow this procedure:

1. Type one or more paragraphs to which you want to add bullets.

2. Select the paragraphs to which you want to add bullets by dragging the mouse over them.

 3. Click the Bullet button in the Formatting toolbar.

To add additional items to the bulleted list, position the cursor at the end of one of the bulleted paragraphs and press Enter. Because the bullet is part of the paragraph format, it carries over to the new paragraph.

The Bullet button works like a toggle: press it once to add bullets, and press it again to remove them. To remove bullets from an entire list, select all the paragraphs in the list and click the Bullet button.

 If you want to create a bulleted list as you go, start by formatting the first paragraph with a bullet; then the bullet format is propagated to subsequent paragraphs as you type them. After you're done, press Enter and then click the Bullet button again to deactivate bullets.

To change the bullet character, choose Format⇨Bullets and Numbering. If the bullet style you want appears in the dialog box, click it and then click OK. Otherwise, click Modify, click Bullet, and then select whichever oddball bullet character makes you happy.

For more information, see Chapter 4 in *MORE Word For Windows 6 For Dummies*.

Lists: Creating a Numbered List

To create a numbered list, follow this procedure:

1. Type one or more paragraphs that you want to number.

2. Select them all.

 3. Click the Numbering button in the Formatting toolbar.

When you add or delete a paragraph in the middle of the list, Word renumbers the paragraphs to preserve the order. When you add a paragraph to the end of the list, Word assigns the next number in sequence to the new paragraph.

The Numbering button works like a toggle: click it once to add numbers to paragraphs, and click it again to remove them. To remove numbering from a numbered paragraph, select the paragraph and click the Numbering button. To remove numbering from an entire list, select all the paragraphs in the list and click the Numbering button.

TIP If you insert a nonnumbered paragraph in the middle of a numbered list, Word breaks the list in two and begins numbering from one again for the second list. However, if you simply turn off numbering for one of the paragraphs in a list, Word suspends the numbering for that paragraph and picks up where it left off with the next numbered paragraph.

For more information, see Chapter 4 in *MORE Word For Windows 6 For Dummies.*

Macros: Recording a Macro

To record a macro, follow these steps:

1. Think about what you're going to do. Rehearse it to make sure that you know what you're doing.

2. Choose the Tools⇨Macro command to summon the Macro dialog box.

3. Name the macro you want to create.

4. Click the Record button. The Record Macro dialog box appears.

5. If you want to make your macro accessible from a toolbar, a menu, or the keyboard, click the <u>T</u>oolbars, <u>M</u>enus, or <u>K</u>eyboard button. Assign the shortcut and then click Close.

6. Click OK to begin recording the macro. A little macro recorder toolbox appears, as shown here.

7. Type the keystrokes and menu commands you want to record in the macro. Click the Pause button in the macro toolbox if you need to temporarily suspend recording; click it again to resume.

 8. After you finish, click the Stop button.

If the macro doesn't work, you may have made a mistake while recording it. Record it again.

Macros are normally stored in global Normal.dot template. To store a macro in the template that's attached to the current document, change the setting of the Record Macro dialog box's Make Macro <u>A</u>vailable To drop-down list.

For more information, see Chapter 16 in *MORE Word For Windows 6 For Dummies.*

Macros: Running a Macro

If you didn't assign a button, menu, or keyboard shortcut to a macro, you have to run it from the <u>T</u>ools⇨<u>M</u>acro command. Here's the procedure:

1. Invoke the <u>T</u>ools⇨<u>M</u>acro command to access the Macro dialog box.

2. Select the macro you want to run from the list of macros currently available.

3. Click Run.

If the macro you want to run doesn't show up in the list, try checking the Macros Available In setting. The macro may be in a different template.

For more information, see Chapter 16 in *MORE Word For Windows 6 For Dummies*.

Mail Merge: Printing Form Letters

Mail Merge is one of the most tedious of all Word tasks. Fortunately, the Mail Merge Helper stands by, ready to help you at a moment's notice. Mail Merge is a three-step process: first, you create the form letter (in WordSpeak, the *main document*); then you create a mailing list of names and addresses (the *data source*); and finally, you merge the form letter and the mailing list to create a letter for each person on your mailing list. The following sections spell out the procedures for each step in detail.

Creating the main document

Here's the procedure for creating a main document to use in a mail merge:

1. Call up the Tools⬩Mail Merge command. The Mail Merge Helper dialog box appears:

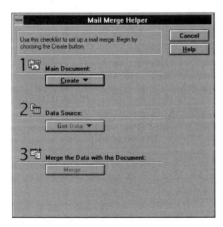

2. Click the Create button and then select Form Letters from the menu that appears. The following dialog box pops up:

3. Click the New Main Document button.

4. Click the Edit button (this button appears on the Mail Merge Helper dialog box after you complete step 3). The Edit button reveals a menu of documents you can edit, but the menu should have only one entry, named *Form Letter: Document #*. Click this selection to edit the letter.

5. Type the letter any way you want, but leave blanks where you want Word to insert personalized data later, such as in the inside address or the salutation ("Dear John…"):

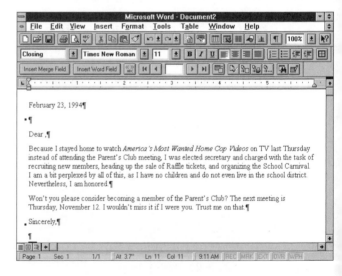

6. Use the File⇨Save command to save the file after you're done.

Creating the data source

The next big step in Mail Merge is creating the data source. This is the hardest part because it requires you to type in all the names and addresses to which you want the form letter sent. Here is the bothersome procedure:

1. Call up the Tools⇔Mail Merge command. The Mail Merge Helper dialog box returns to life:

2. Click the Get Data button and then choose Create Data Source from the menu that appears. You then see the Create Data Source dialog box:

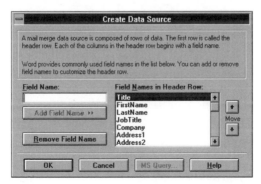

3. If you want, you can add or remove fields included in the data source. To remove a field, click the field to select it

and then click the Remove Field Name button. To add a
field, type a name in the Field Name box and click the Add
Field Name button. To change the order in which the fields
appear, click the field you want to move to select it and then
click the up-arrow or down-arrow button to move the field.

4. Click OK when you're satisfied with the fields to be included
   in the data source.

5. When Word displays the Save Data Source dialog box, type
   an appropriate name to save your mailing list document
   and then click OK. This dialog box appears:

6. Click the Edit Data Source button to begin adding names
   and addresses to the data source. A Data Form dialog box
   similar to the one shown here appears:

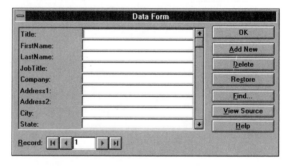

7. Type the information for one person you want to add to the
   data source. Use the Tab key to move from field to field or
   to skip over those fields you don't want to enter (you don't
   have to enter a value for every field).

8. After you type all the data for the person, click Add New to
   add that person's data to the table in the data source.

9. Repeat steps 7 and 8 for each person that you want to add
   to the data source.

10. After you've added all the names that you want to add, click OK.

Note that you can use the arrow buttons at the bottom of the Data Source dialog box to move forward or backward through the data source records. Thus, you can recall a previously entered record to correct a mistake if necessary.

To delete a record, use the arrow buttons at the bottom of the Data Source dialog box to move to the record you want to delete and then click Delete.

Inserting field names in the main document

After you finish adding names and addresses to the data source, return to the main document. Now it is time to add field names to the main document so that Word knows where to insert data from the data source into the form letter. Here's the procedure:

1. Position the insertion point where you want to insert a field from the data source.

2. Click the Insert Merge Field button in the Mail Merge toolbar. A menu of field names from the data source appears:

3. Click the field that you want to insert into the document.

4. Repeat steps 1 through 3 for each field that you want to insert. Remember that the fields themselves do not contain any punctuation or spacing, so be sure to type any necessary punctuation or spacing in the document before inserting the fields. The next figure shows what a document looks like with all the fields inserted.

5. After you're finished, use the File⇨Save command to save the file.

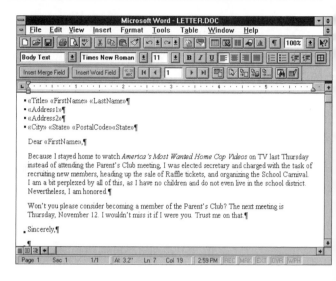

Merging the documents

Now that you've set up the main document and the data source, you're ready for the show. Follow these simple steps to merge the main document with the data source to produce form letters:

1. Use the Tools➪Mail Merge command to summon the Mail Merge Helper.

2. Click the Merge button. The Merge dialog box appears:

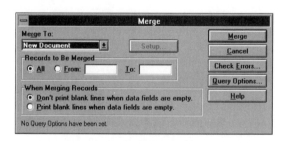

3. Click the Merge button.

Word creates a new document that contains one complete copy of the main document for each record in the data source, with data from the data source substituted for each merge field. The merged copies are separated from one another by section breaks.

4. Review the merged document to make sure that the merge worked the way you expected.

5. If you want to save the merged document, use the File⇨Save command. It's a good idea to save the file, but be warned that the file may be quite large, depending on how many records you merged from the data source.

6. To print the merged document, choose File⇨Print.

Replace: *Replacing Text*

You can use the Edit⇨Replace command to replace all occurrences of one bit of text with other text. Here's the procedure:

1. Press Ctrl+Home to get to the top of the document. If you skip this step, the search-and-replace operation will start at the position of the insertion point.

2. Choose Edit⇨Replace or press Ctrl+H to summon the Replace dialog box:

3. Type the text you want to find in the Find What field, and type the text you want to substitute for the Find What text in the Replace With field.

4. Click the Find Next button. When Word finds the text, it highlights it on-screen.

5. Click the Replace button to replace the text.

6. Repeat the Find Next and Replace sequence until you're finished.

As for the Find command, you can use the Match Case, Find Whole Word Only, Use Pattern Matching, and Sounds Like options. See the procedure "Finding Text" earlier in this part for details.

If you're absolutely positive that you want to replace all occurrences of your Fi_n_d What text with the Re_p_lace With text, click the Replace _A_ll button. This step automatically replaces all remaining occurrences of the text. The only problem is that you're bound to encounter at least one spot where you don't want the replacement to occur. Replacing the word *mit* with *glove*, for example, changes Smith to Sgloveh (and no, *Sgloveh* is not the Czechoslovakian form of the name *Smith*).

If you do click the Replace _A_ll button, Word displays an informative message after it finishes, indicating how many replacements were made:

Spell: Checking Your Spelling

The spelling checker is one of Word's most useful commands, especially if you're running for Vice Presidente. Here's how to use it:

1. Call up the _T_ools⇨_S_pelling command, press F7, or click the Spelling button. Whichever you choose, Word begins checking your spelling.

2. When Word finds a misspelled word, it displays the Spelling dialog box:

3. If the word really is misspelled, choose the correct spelling from the list of suggested spellings that appears in the dialog box and click the _C_hange button. If the correct spelling doesn't appear among the suggestions, type the correct spelling in the Change _T_o field and click the _C_hange button.

If the word is correctly spelled as it is, click the Ignore button. Sometimes this happens. In the preceding figure, the word *Accreditations* is spelled correctly but isn't in Word's spelling dictionary. (You may think that I'm crazy to use a word like Accreditations in the first place, but I actually created the document by using Word's built-in Resume Wizard. The Resume Wizard put that word in the document by itself, but Microsoft forgot to add the word to the spelling dictionary!)

4. Repeat steps 2 and 3 until Word gives up and displays the following message:

Styles: Applying a Style

To apply a style to a paragraph, follow these steps:

1. Put the cursor in the paragraph you want to format (it isn't necessary to highlight the entire paragraph).

2. Select the style you want from the style box in the Formatting toolbar.

To apply a style to two or more adjacent paragraphs, just select a range of text that includes all the paragraphs you want to format. Then select the style.

Every paragraph in a document is assigned a style. The default style for the first paragraph in a new document is called *Normal*.

You can tell which style is assigned to a paragraph by clicking anywhere in the paragraph and looking at the style box. It shows the name of the style assigned to that paragraph.

If the style you're looking for doesn't appear in the style list, hold down the Shift key and click the down arrow next to the style box. Sometimes Word doesn't list all the styles that are available until you do so.

To quickly return a paragraph to Normal style, press Ctrl+Shift+N. To assign the built-in Heading 1, Heading 2, or Heading 3 styles, press Ctrl+Alt+1, Ctrl+Alt+2, or Ctrl+Alt+3, respectively (assuming that you haven't reassigned these keyboard shortcuts by using the Tools⇨Customize command).

For more information, see Chapter 14 in *Word For Windows 6 For Dummies* or Chapter 2 in *MORE Word For Windows 6 For Dummies*.

Styles: Creating a Style

To create a new style, follow these steps:

1. Tweak a paragraph until it is formatted just the way you want. Set the font and size, line spacing, before and after spacing, and indentation. Also set tabs and any other formatting you want, such as bullets or numbers.

2. Press Ctrl+Shift+S or click the style box in the Formatting toolbar (the style box is the leftmost box in the Formatting toolbar).

3. Type a descriptive name for the style.

4. Press Enter to add the style to Word's list of styles for the document.

For more information, see Chapter 14 in *Word For Windows 6 For Dummies* or Chapter 2 in *MORE Word For Windows 6 For Dummies*.

Table of Authorities: Inserting a Table of Authorities

If you use Word to create legal documents, you'll appreciate the Table of Authorities feature. Using it is a two-phase process: first, you must mark any citations you want to include in the table. Then you create the table itself.

Marking citations

To mark a citation, follow this procedure:

1. Highlight the citation you want to mark and press Alt+Shift+I. The Mark Citation dialog box appears:

Mark Citation	
Selected Text: Kringle v. New York 28 NY 2d 312 (1938)	Next Citation Cancel
Category: Cases	Mark
Short Citation: Kringle v. New York, 28 NY 2d 312 (1938)	Mark All Category... Help
Long Citation	

2. If the citation in the document is not as it should appear in the table of authorities, click in the Selected <u>T</u>ext field and type the citation exactly as you want it to appear in the table. If you want to split the citation into two lines, just position the cursor where you want the line to be split and press Enter.

3. The first time you cite an authority, you must provide a complete citation (such as "*Kringle v. New York,* 28 NY 2d 312 (1938)"), but thereafter you use the short form ("*Kringle v. New York*"). Edit the <u>S</u>hort Citation field to match the short form of the citation so that Word will automatically locate subsequent citations and mark them.

4. Select the type of authority being cited from the <u>C</u>ategory list box.

5. Click <u>M</u>ark to mark the citation. Word inserts a hidden field code to mark the citation.

6. The Mark Citation dialog box stays on-screen so you can mark additional citations. Click the <u>N</u>ext Citation button to find the next citation. The <u>N</u>ext Citation button searches for text, such as *v,* that is commonly found in citations.

7. Highlight the complete text of the citation found by the <u>N</u>ext Citation button. The <u>N</u>ext Citation button doesn't highlight the complete citation; it highlights only the text that convinced it to stop because a citation is probably nearby. Use the mouse to highlight the complete citation in the document.

8. Repeat steps 3 through 7 until you've marked all the citations you can stand.

9. When you're done marking citations, click the Cancel button.

Inserting the table

After the citations are marked, you can use the following procedure to create a table of authorities:

1. Move the insertion point to the place where you want the table of authorities to appear.

2. Call up the <u>I</u>nsert⇨Inde<u>x</u> and Tables command and click the Table of <u>A</u>uthorities tab. The Index and Tables dialog box appears with the table of authorities options in plain view.

3. Pick the style you want from the Forma<u>t</u>s list.

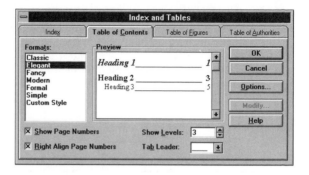

4. Play with the other controls to fine-tune the table of authorities:

- **Use Passim:** Check this option if you want Word to use the word *Passim* when a citation occurs on five or more pages. (*Passim* is a Latin word that means *scattered throughout* — it has nothing to do with an ugly overgrown rat-like creature that hangs upside down by its tail.)

- **Keep Original Formatting:** Check this option if you want character formatting (like underline, italic, and so on) applied to the citation as it appears in the document to be carried over into the table of authorities.

- **Category:** Select the citation category you want compiled. Usually, you should leave this field set to the default, All. If you want to compile a table of one category (cases, rules, regulations, and so on), select the category from the drop-down list.

- **Tab Leader:** Select the tab leader style you want to use.

5. Click OK to create the table of authorities.

Table of Contents: Inserting a Table of Contents

To create a table of contents, make sure that you format your document's headings by using Word's heading styles (Heading 1, Heading 2, and Heading 3). If you do, creating a table of contents is easy. Here's the procedure:

1. Move the insertion point to the place where you want the table of contents to appear.

2. Call up the Insert⇨Index and Tables command and click the Table of Contents tab. The Index and Tables dialog box appears.

3. Pick the Table of Contents style you want from the Formats list.

4. Play with the other controls to fine-tune the table of contents:

   - **Show Page Numbers:** Uncheck this box if you want the TOC to show the document's outline but not page numbers.

   - **Right Align Page Numbers:** Uncheck this box if you want the page numbers to be placed right next to the corresponding text rather than at the right margin.

   - **Show Levels:** Use this control to set the amount of detail included in the table.

   - **Tab Leader:** Select the tab leader style you want to use.

5. Click OK. The TOC is inserted into the document.

If the table of contents looks like {TOC \o "1-3" \p " "}, call up the Tools⇨Options command, click the View button, and uncheck the Field Codes checkbox. Click OK and the table will appear as it should.

To regenerate a table of contents, select the table by clicking anywhere in it with the mouse and then press F9.

The entries in a TOC are formatted with a set of standard styles named TOC 1, TOC 2, TOC 3, and so on. If you don't like any of the predefined formats listed in the Formats list, select Custom Style and click the Modify button. Doing so takes you to a special version of the Style dialog box in which only the standard TOC styles are shown. You can then change the appearance of the Custom Style Table of Contents format by modifying the various TOC styles.

Tables: Creating a Table

To create a beautifully formatted table, follow this procedure:

1. Position the insertion point where you want to insert the table.

2. Call up the Table⇨Insert Table command. The Insert Table dialog box appears.

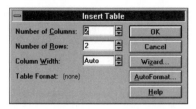

3. Click the Wizard button. The Table Wizard dialog box appears:

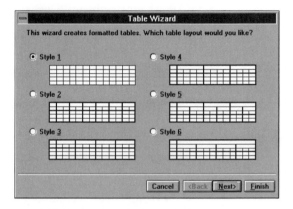

4. Select the table style you want.

5. Click Next>.

6. From the next Table Wizard screen, select the type of table column headings you want to use. Notice that the selection you make here also determines how many columns appear in the table.

7. Click Next>. The Table Wizard continues.

8. Answer the annoying questions about whether you want the headings repeated on each page (only important for long tables) and whether you want the column headings left-aligned, centered, or right-aligned.

9. Click Next>. The Table Wizard continues:

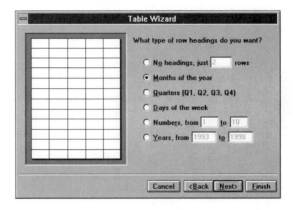

10. Select the type of table row headings you want to use. In the preceding example, I selected the months of the year to use for row headings. Note that the selection you make here also determines how many rows appear in the table.

11. Click Next>.

12. From the next Table Wizard screen, select the alignment for the row headings: left, centered, or right.

13. Click Next>. The Table Wizard continues:

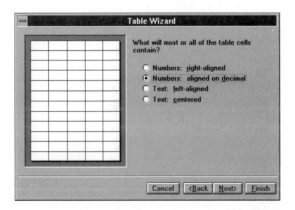

14. Select the alignment for the data that appears in the table cells. You can choose from two numeric formats (right-aligned or decimal-aligned) or two text formats (left-aligned or centered).

15. Click Next>.

16. Select whether you want the table to use Portrait or Landscape orientation.

17. Click Next>.

18. Finally! Tell the Table Wizard whether or not you need help after the table is created and then click Finish.

19. Stretch your muscles for a moment, but don't leave your computer. In just a moment, the Table AutoFormat dialog box appears:

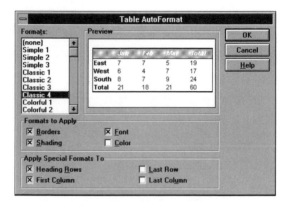

20. Select the formatting you want to apply to the table and then click OK.

Here's what the finished product should look like:

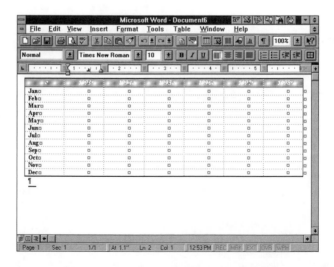

Tabs: Creating Leader Tabs

Leader tabs have rows of dots instead of spaces between tab stops. They're used in tables of contents or indexes. Here's the procedure for creating them:

1. Set a tab stop by using the "Setting Tabs" procedure.

2. Call up the Format➪Tabs command. The Tabs dialog box appears.

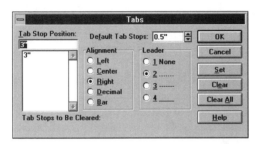

3. Choose the leader style by using option 2, 3, or 4.

4. Click OK.

Now, when you press the Tab key, a row of dots or a solid line appears.

For more information, see Chapter 10 in *Word For Windows 6 For Dummies* or Chapter 1 in *MORE Word For Windows 6 For Dummies*.

Tabs: Setting Tab Stops

Here's the procedure for setting tabs with the ruler:

1. Type some text that you want to line up with tab stops.

2. Select the paragraph or paragraphs whose tabs you want to set.

3. Click the ruler at each spot where you want a new tab stop.

4. Adjust the settings until you like the way the text looks.

To adjust a tab setting, just grab the tab marker in the ruler with the mouse and slide it to the new location. (If you can't find the ruler, choose View➪Ruler to display it.) When you release the mouse button, text in the currently selected paragraphs adjusts to the new tab position.

Default tab stops are placed every .5 inch. However, each time you create a new tab stop, all default tab stops to the left of the new tab stop are deleted. In other words, default tab stops exist only to the right of tab stops you create.

Word lets you create four types of tab alignments: left, center, right, and decimal. To change the type of tab that's created when you click the ruler, click the Tab Alignment Button at the far-left edge of the ruler. Each time you click, the picture on the button changes to indicate the alignment type:

⌊	Left tab: Text is left-aligned at the tab stop.
⌶	Center tab: Text is centered over the tab stop.
⌐	Right tab: Text is right-aligned over the tab stop.
⌐	Decimal tab: Numbers are aligned at the decimal point over the tab stops.

To remove a tab stop from the ruler, click the tab stop you want to remove and drag it straight down off the ruler. When you release the mouse, the tab stop is deleted.

To quickly remove all tab stops, issue the Format⇨Tabs command and then click the Clear All button.

For more information, see Chapter 10 in *Word For Windows 6 For Dummies* or Chapter 1 in *MORE Word For Windows 6 For Dummies*.

Templates: Creating a New Template

Suppose you've toiled for hours on a document, and now you want to make its styles available to other documents you may someday create. The simplest solution is to create a template that contains the styles in your document. Here's how:

1. Open the document that has all the styles you want to save in a template.

2. Choose File⇨Save As.

3. Way down at the bottom of the Save As dialog box, find the Save File as Type box. Select Document Template as the file type.

4. Type a filename for the template (don't type the extension; let Word take care of it).

5. Click OK to save the document as a template file.

6. Delete unnecessary text from the file.

7. Save the file again.

Another way to create a template is to use the File⇨New command and then click the Template check box in the New dialog box. Doing so creates an empty template based on the template you select in the dialog box. You can them modify the template as you see fit and save it under a new name.

For more information, see Chapter 15 in *Word For Windows 6 For Dummies* or Chapter 3 in *MORE Word For Windows 6 For Dummies.*

Thesaurus: Using the Thesaurus

Word's Thesaurus enables you to spice up your prose by looking up synonyms. Here's the procedure:

1. Select the word you want to look up. (You don't have to select the entire word; just click the word with the mouse so that the insertion point sits within the word.)

2. Call up the Tools⇨Thesaurus command or use the keyboard shortcut Shift+F7. Either way, the Thesaurus dialog box appears.

3. If more than one category of Meanings appears on the left side of the dialog box, click the one you're interested in.

4. If one of the words that appears is close to the meaning you're looking for, click it to select it and then click the Look Up button. This action often yields additional words that may be of interest. You can continue in this fashion as long as you want.

5. When you find the word you want to use, click it to select it and then click Replace. The word replaces the selected word in your document.

Part III

Excel

This part covers the spreadsheet of spreadsheets, Excel 5. Excel is far too complicated a program to present all its intricacies in this little book, so this part covers just the basics. You can find a lot more information in *Excel For Dummies,* Second Edition and *MORE Excel For Dummies.*

The Excel Screen

The following figure shows you what Excel's screen looks like when you're editing a worksheet.

In the center of the screen is the main document window, which displays the Excel workbook file you're working with. (Yes, even though Excel files are called *workbooks* rather than *documents,* the main window is still called a *document window.* Stupid is as stupid does.) In this example, only one workbook file is open, and its window is maximized so that it fills all the space available within the document window. However, you can open more than one workbook file and display the files at the same time in separately sizable document windows.

The formula bar shows the current cell address and the contents of the cell. In this example, cell A1 contains the text *BLUE SKY AIRLINES.* Excel uses the same letter-number scheme to refer to cells as other spreadsheet programs: it gives each column in the worksheet a letter and each row a number. Thus cell A1 is at the intersection of column A and row 1, and cell G30 is at the intersection of column G and row 30.

Formula bar

MOM

Microsoft Excel - SALES.XLS

File   Edit   View   Insert   Format   Tools   Data   Window   Help

Times New Roman   12   **B** *I* U $ % ,   100%

A1   BLUE SKY AIRLINES

	A	B	C	D	E	F	G	H	I
1	BLUE SKY AIRLINES								
2	Sales Report								
3									
4		Region	January	February					
5		North	10111	13400					
6		South	22100	24050					
7		East	13270	15670					
8		West	10800	21500					
9									
10									
11									
12									
13									
14									
15									
16									
17									
18									

Sales Report / Sheet2 / Sheet3 / Sheet4 / Sheet5 / S

Ready   NUM

Mode indicator   Sheet tabs

Tab scroll buttons

A worksheet can be as large as 256 columns and 16,384 rows. You can easily account for 16,384 rows by using numbers, but how do you account for 256 columns by using letters? Excel manages by doubling the letters. The columns that follow column Z are columns AA, AB, AC, and so on, all the way up to AZ. After column AZ come columns BA, BB, BC, and so on, up to BZ, CA, CB, CC, and so on. The last possible column in a worksheet is IV, which is appropriate — anyone who would build a worksheet with that many columns is probably in need of medical attention.

Each workbook file contains one or more *worksheets.* When you first create a workbook, it contains 16 blank worksheets. However, you can easily add or remove worksheets. A workbook can contain as many worksheets as can fit in your computer's memory. The sheet tabs let you quickly call up a different worksheet within the same workbook file. When you want to work on a worksheet, click its tab to bring the worksheet to the front.

Many workbooks contain more sheets than can be shown in the small area allotted for sheet tabs. The arrow buttons to the left of the sheet tabs let you scroll through a workbook's sheet tabs.

Roll Call of Keyboard Shortcuts

Excel has more keyboard shortcuts than you can possibly remember. Here are the more important ones.

Formatting

Shortcut	What It Does
Ctrl+1	Calls up the Format Cells dialog box so that you can apply cell formatting.
Ctrl+B	**Bolds** selected text.
Ctrl+I	*Italicizes* selected text.
Ctrl+U	<u>Underlines</u> selected text.
Ctrl+Shift+~	Applies general number style.
Ctrl+Shift+$	Applies currency number style.
Ctrl+Shift+%	Applies percent number style.
Ctrl+Shift+^	Applies exponential number style.
Ctrl+Shift+#	Applies date number style.
Ctrl+Shift+@	Applies time number style.
Ctrl+Shift+!	Applies comma number style.
Ctrl+Shift+&	Adds an outline border.
Ctrl+Shift+_	Removes outline borders.

Entering and Editing Data

Shortcut	What It Does
Ctrl+X	Cuts text to the Clipboard.
Ctrl+C	Copies text to the Clipboard.
Ctrl+V	Pastes text from the Clipboard.
Ctrl+Z	Undoes the last action.
Ctrl+F	Finds text.
Ctrl+H	Replaces text.
Ctrl+A	Selects everything in a worksheet.

(continues)

Shortcut	What It Does
Ctrl+D	Fills the selected range of cells down, using the values at the top of the range to determine the sequence of values to be used.
Ctrl+R	Fills the selected range of cells right, using the values at the left of the range to determine the sequence of values to be used.
Ctrl+;	Enters the current date.
Ctrl+Shift+:	Enters the current time.

File Management

Shortcut	What It Does
Ctrl+N	Creates a new file.
Ctrl+O	Opens an existing file.
Ctrl+S	Saves a file.
F12	Saves a file using a new filename.
Ctrl+P	Prints the file.
Alt+F4	Exits Excel.
Ctrl+F6	Switches to the next document window in sequence.
Ctrl+Shift+F6	Switches to the preceding document window in sequence.

Navigating

Shortcut	What It Does
Home	Moves to the beginning of the current row.
PgUp	Scrolls the window up one screen.
PgDn	Scrolls the window down one screen.
Alt+PgDn	Scrolls the window right one screen.
Alt+PgUp	Scrolls the window left one screen.
Ctrl+End	Moves to the last cell of worksheet that contains data.

(continues)

Ctrl+Home	Moves to the beginning of the worksheet.
Ctrl+← or End, ←	Moves to the left of a data block.
Ctrl+→ or End, →	Moves to the right of a data block.
Ctrl+↑ or End, ↑	Moves to the top of a data block
Ctrl+↓ or End, ↓	Moves to the bottom of a data block.
Ctrl+PgUp	Switches to the preceding sheet in the same workbook.
Ctrl+PgDn	Switches to the next sheet in the same workbook.
End, Home	Moves to the last cell in the worksheet that contains data.
End, Enter	Moves to the last cell in the current row that contains data.
Ctrl+G	Goes to a specific location.

To highlight cells, hold down the Shift key while using these keyboard shortcuts (except Ctrl+G) or press F2. You can also click and drag the mouse across the cells that you want to highlight.

Besides holding down Shift while navigating or dragging the mouse, several shortcut keys for selecting cells are available.

Selecting Cells

Shortcut	What It Does
Ctrl+spacebar	Selects the entire column.
Shift+spacebar	Selects the entire row.
Ctrl+Shift+spacebar or Ctrl+A	Selects the entire worksheet.
Ctrl+Shift+*	Selects the entire block of data.
Ctrl+Shift+?	Selects all cells that have a note attached.

Favorite Excel Functions

Excel provides about a million functions that you can incorporate into your formulas. You can find a complete list of functions in the on-line help or via the Function Wizard. This section lists the most commonly used functions.

ABS

```
ABS(number)
```

Returns the absolute value of *number*.

AVERAGE

```
AVERAGE(range)
```

Calculates the average value of the cells in *range* by adding up the sum of the cells and then dividing the result by the number of cells in the range. Blank cells are not counted, but cells that contain the value zero are.

COUNT

```
COUNT(range)
```

Returns the number of cells in *range*. Blank cells are not counted, but cells that contain the value zero are.

HLOOKUP

```
HLOOKUP(lookup_value, table_array,
row_index_num)
```

Searches for the cell in *table_array* that contains the value specified by *lookup_value*. HLOOKUP searches all the cells in the first row of the range specified for *table_array*. If it finds *lookup_value*, HLOOKUP returns the value of the corresponding cell in the row indicated by *row_index_num*. For example, to return the value in the corresponding cell in the second row of the table, specify 2 for *row_index_num*.

IF

```
IF(logical_test, value_if_true,
value_if_false)
```

Tests the condition spelled out in the logical test. If the condition is true, Excel returns *value_if_true*. Otherwise, it returns *value_if_false*.

LOWER

```
LOWER(text)
```

Converts the text to lowercase.

MAXIMUM

```
MAXIMUM(range)
```

Returns the largest value in *range*.

MEDIAN

```
MEDIAN(range)
```

Returns the median value of the cells in *range*. When you sort the cells in order, the median value is the value in the cell that falls right in the middle of the sorted list. Half the cell values are larger than the median value, and the other half are smaller.

MINIMUM

```
MINIMUM(range)
```

Returns the smallest value in *range*.

NOW

```
NOW()
```

Returns the current date and time. No arguments are required.

PMT

    PMT(rate, nper, pv, fv, type)

Calculates payments for a loan. *Rate* is the interest rate per period; *nper* is the number of periods; *pv* is the present value (that is, the amount of the loan). *Fv* and *type* represent the future value and loan type (0 = payments made at the end of each period, and 1 = payments made at the beginning of each period) and are rarely used. Be sure to specify the interest rate for each period and the total number of periods. For example, if the annual interest rate is 12 percent and you make payments monthly, the periodic interest rate is 1 percent. Likewise, if the loan is for three years and you make payments monthly, there are 36 periods.

PRODUCT

    PRODUCT(range)

Multiplies all the cells in the specified range.

PROPER

    PROPER(text)

Converts the text to proper case, in which the first letter of each word is capitalized.

ROUND

    ROUND(number, digits)

Rounds off the *number* to the specified number of *digits*. For example, ROUND(C1,2) rounds off the value in cell C1 to two decimal places.

SUM

    SUM(range)

Adds the values of all cells in the specified range.

SUMPRODUCT

```
SUMPRODUCT(range1, range2)
```

Multiplies each cell in *range1* by its corresponding cell in *range2* and then adds the resulting products together.

TODAY

```
TODAY()
```

Returns the current date. No arguments are required.

UPPER

```
UPPER(text)
```

Converts the text to uppercase.

VLOOKUP

```
VLOOKUP(lookup_value, table_array,
col_index_num)
```

Searches for the cell in *table_array* that contains the value specified by *lookup_value*. VLOOKUP searches all the cells in the first column of the range specified for *table_array*. If it finds *lookup_value,* VLOOKUP returns the value of the corresponding cell in the column indicated by *col_index_num*. For example, to return the value in the corresponding cell in the second column of the table, specify **2** for *col_index_num*.

Best Loved Procedures

This section contains a hodge-podge of procedures for working with various aspects of Excel.

Charts: Creating a Chart

Excel's charting capabilities are the subject for a separate book.
Here's the short procedure for quickly creating a simple chart:

1. Select the cells that contain the data on which you want to
   base a chart.

2. Click the ChartWizard button in the Standard toolbar. The
   cursor changes into a little crosshair.

3. Drag the crosshair pointer to mark the location where you
   want the chart inserted and designate its size. As you drag
   the pointer, a rectangle indicates the size and position of
   the chart.

4. Release the mouse button to call up the Chart Wizard.

5. In Step 1 of the Chart Wizard, verify that you marked the
   correct cells for the data to be charted:

6. Click Next > to continue to the next step.

7. In Step 2 of the Chart Wizard, select the chart type that you
   want to use:

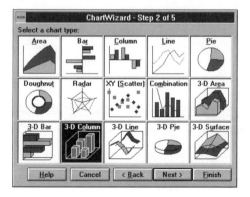

8. Click Next > to continue to the next step.

9. In Step 3 of the Chart Wizard, select the format for the chart type you picked:

10. Click Next > to continue to the next step.

11. In Step 4 of the Chart Wizard, you see a preview of the charted data. Normally, each column of data is charted as a separate data series; if the chart looks all fouled up, click Rows to chart each row as a data series. Also, you can tell the Chart Wizard to use the first row or column for the X-axis labels or the Y-axis labels:

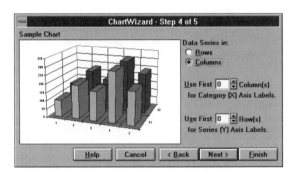

12. Click Next > to continue to the next step.

13. In Step 5 of the Chart Wizard, you can add legends or titles to the chart.

14. After you're done adding legends and titles, click Finish to complete the chart.

When the chart is complete, you can use the tools in the Chart toolbar to tweak the chart's appearance.

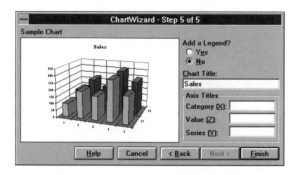

To change the size or location of the chart, click it and drag one of its corner handles.

Double-click a chart to change the various elements that make up the chart. You can then double-click the different parts of the chart to bring up various dialog boxes that let you tweak the chart's appearance.

To delete a chart, click it to select it and press Delete.

For more information, see Chapter 7 in *Excel For Dummies, Second Edition.*

Fill: Creating and Using a Custom Series

Excel's AutoFill command is adept at filling a range of cells with a series of numbers (1, 2, 3, . . .) or dates (January, February, March, . . .). But what if you routinely find yourself entering an oddball series of text entries, such as the names of your top sales reps (Doc, Grumpy, Bashful, . . .)? Excel lets you create your own custom series, so you only have to type the first text entry (**Doc**) in a cell and then drag the cell's fill handle down the column or across the row.

Follow these steps to create your own custom series:

1. Choose the Tools⇨Options command.

2. In the Options dialog box, click the Custom Lists tab.

3. Click the List Entries box and then type your list. The following figure shows what the Options dialog box looks like after you enter the sales rep list.

4. Click Add. The list is added to the Custom Lists box in the form.

5. Click OK to dismiss the Options dialog box.

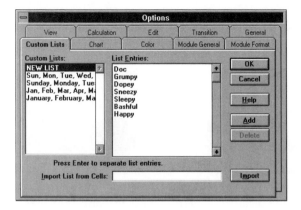

To insert a previously defined custom list into a worksheet, follow these steps:

1. Type one of the text entries from the list in a cell.

2. Grab the fill handle (the small box at the bottom right of the cell) and drag it to mark the range of cells into which you want to insert the list.

3. Release the mouse button, and the list is inserted.

If the contents of the first cell are repeated in each cell, you probably typed the cell value incorrectly. Double-check it and try again.

To delete a custom list, choose Tools⇨Options, click the Custom Lists tab, select the list, and click Delete. To correct an error in a list, delete the list and re-create it.

You can also create a list from text entries stored in a range of worksheet cells. Type the list in a column or row of cells and then select the entire list. Choose Tools⇨Options, click the Custom Lists tab, and then click Import.

For more information, see Chapter 2 in *Excel For Dummies,* Second Edition.

Find: Finding Lost Data

You can use the Edit⇨Find command to find text anywhere in a worksheet. Just follow these steps:

1. Press Ctrl+Home to move to the top of the worksheet. This step is optional; if you omit it, the search starts at the current cell.

2. Use the Edit⇨Find command or press Ctrl+F to summon the Find dialog box:

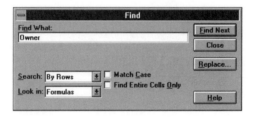

3. Type the text you want to find in the Find What field.

4. Click the Find Next button.

5. When Excel finds the cell that contains the text you're looking for, it highlights the cell. The Find dialog box remains on-screen so you can Click Find Next to find yet another occurrence of the text.

6. When Excel finds the last occurrence of the text, it resumes its search again from the top. This process goes on forever, until you bail out by clicking Cancel or pressing Esc.

You can change the direction of the search by changing the setting for the Search drop-down box. The choices are

- **By Rows:** Searches all the cells of one row before moving on to the next row.

- **By Columns:** Searches all the cells of one column before moving on to the next column.

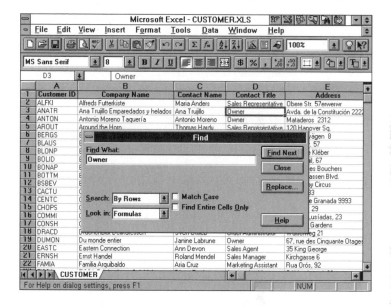

Check the Match Case option before beginning the search if it matters whether the text appears in uppercase or lowercase letters.

If you want to find text only if the entire cell entry matches the Find What text, check the Find Entire Cells Only option.

You can use the following wildcard characters in the Find What text:

- **?** finds a single occurrence of any character. For example, **f?t** finds *fat* and *fit*.

- ***** finds any combination of characters. For example, **b*t** finds any combination of characters that begins with *b* and ends with *t,* such as *bat, bait, ballast,* and *bacteriologist.*

If you find the text you're looking for and decide that you want to replace it with something else, click Replace. Then skip ahead to "Replace: Replacing Data" for details on replacing text.

For more information, see Chapter 5 of *Excel For Dummies,* Second Edition.

Formatting: Centering Text over Several Columns

One of the most useful formatting tricks is centering a text entry over several columns. For example, suppose you have projected net sales for 1993, 1994, and 1995 in columns B, C, and D and actual net sales for 1993, 1994, and 1995 in columns E, F, and G. Wouldn't it be nice to have a *Projected Net Sales* heading centered over the projected net sales columns and an *Actual Net Sales* heading centered over the actual net sales columns, as in the worksheet in the next figure?

Here is the procedure for centering text over several columns:

1. Move the cell pointer to the leftmost cell in the range of columns over which you want the text centered. For example, if you want text centered over the range B3:D3, then move the cell pointer to cell B3.

2. Enter the text that you want centered.

3. Highlight the range of cells over which you want the text centered. The worksheet should now look something like the second figure.

4. Click the Center Across Columns button.

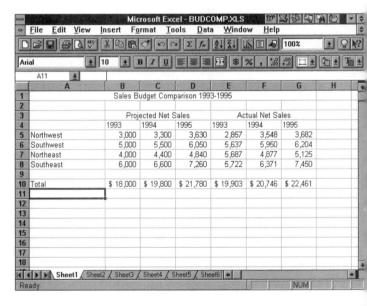

If you change your mind and don't want the text centered across columns, move the cell pointer to the leftmost cell in the range (B3 in this example) and click the Center Across Columns button again.

For more information, see Chapter 3 in *Excel For Dummies, Second Edition.*

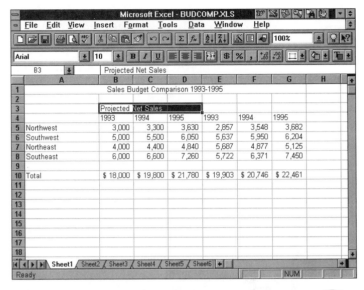

Formatting: Setting the Cell Format

You can set formats for a cell or range of cells by using the formatting keyboard shortcuts listed earlier in this part or by using the formatting controls that are available on the Formatting toolbar. Or you can use the following procedure to apply character formats via the Format⇨Cells command:

1. Highlight the cell or cells to which you want to apply the formatting.

2. Call up the Format⇨Cells command or use the handy keyboard shortcut, Ctrl+1. Either way, the Format Cells dialog box appears:

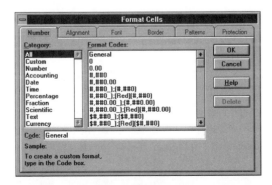

3. Play with the controls to set the formatting options that you want. The options are organized under these six tabs:

Tab	Settings
Number	The number Category (for example, Number, Percentage, or Currency) and the specific Format Codes used to format the number. You can pick from a list of preset format codes or create your own.
Alignment	Horizontal (General, Left, Center, Right, Fill, Justify, Center across selection), Vertical (Top, Center, Bottom, Justify), Wrap Text, and Orientation.
Font	Font, Font style, Size, Underline, Color, Normal font, and Effects (Strikethrough, Superscript, Subscript).
Border	Border (Outline, Left, Right, Top, Bottom), Style, and Color.
Patterns	Color and Pattern.
Protection	Locked and Hidden.

4. Click OK when the cells are formatted the way you want.

For more information, see Chapter 3 of *Excel For Dummies,* Second Edition.

Formatting: Using AutoFormats

You can create an attractively formatted worksheet most efficiently by using the Format⇨AutoFormat command to apply predefined formatting to your worksheet. Here's how:

1. Create your worksheet as you normally would. The Format⇨AutoFormat command works best when the first row and the first column of the worksheet contain headings and the last row contains totals. The last column of the worksheet may also contain totals, but it doesn't have to. The Auto-Formats work whether or not the last column contains totals.

2. Highlight the entire range of worksheet cells that contains data you want formatted, as in the following:

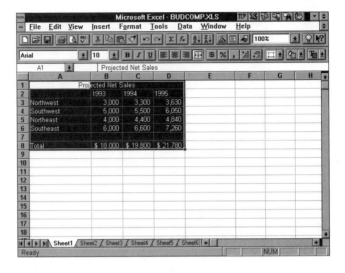

3. Call up the Format⇨AutoFormat command. The AutoFormat dialog box appears:

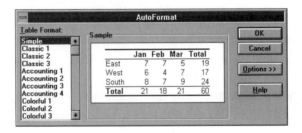

4. Select the Table Format you want to use. A preview of each AutoFormat appears in the Sample portion of the AutoFormat dialog box.

5. Click OK. The AutoFormat is applied.

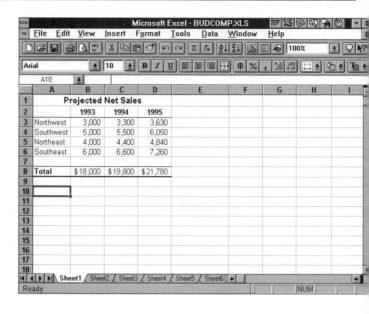

Examine the results of the AutoFormat before using any other Excel command. If you don't like the formatting, press Ctrl+Z to undo the AutoFormat operation.

For more information, see Chapter 3 in *Excel For Dummies, Second Edition.*

Functions: Using the Function Wizard

The easiest way to insert a function is to use the Function Wizard. The Function Wizard asks you to select a function from one of several function categories and to complete the function by providing all arguments that the function requires.

Here is the procedure, using a simple MAX function as an example:

1. Move the cell pointer to the cell in which you want to insert the function:

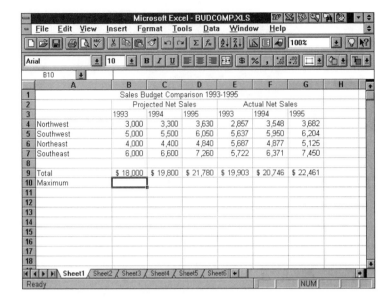

2. Call up the Insert⇨Function command. The Function Wizard appears:

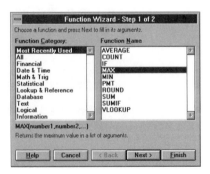

3. Initially, the Function Wizard lists the functions you've used most recently. If the function you want to insert is listed in the Function Name list, click it to select it. Otherwise, click one of the categories in the Function Category list and then select the function from the Function Name list.

4. Click Next >. Step 2 of the Function Wizard appears:

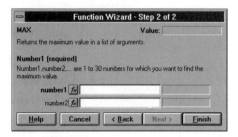

5. Read the instructions for completing the function and then type whatever entries are required to complete the function.

   If the function requires you to enter a range of cells, you can mark the cells directly in the worksheet. You may need to move the Function Wizard dialog box to make the cells visible, as the following figure shows:

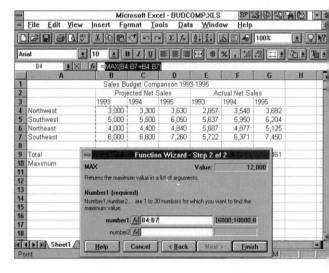

6. Click **F**inish after you complete the function. Here is what the MAX function looks like when completed:

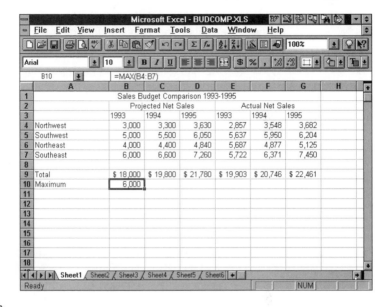

For more information about specific functions, see the "Favorite Excel Functions" section earlier in this part.

For more information, see Chapter 2 of *Excel For Dummies,* Second Edition.

Macros: Recording a Macro

To record a macro, follow these steps:

1. Think about what you're going to do. Rehearse it to make sure that you know what you're doing.

2. Choose Tools⇨Record Macro⇨Record New Macro to summon the Record New Macro dialog box.

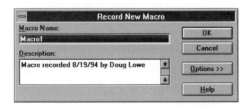

3. Type a name for the macro that you want to create.

4. If you want to assign the macro to a keyboard shortcut or put it in the Tools menu, click the <u>O</u>ptions button and complete the appropriate dialog box settings. If you want the macro to be available no matter which workbook is open, select the <u>P</u>ersonal Macro Workbook option.

5. Click OK to begin recording the macro.

6. Type the keystrokes and menu commands that you want to record in the macro.

 7. After you're done, click the Stop button.

If the macro doesn't work, you may have made a mistake while recording it. Try recording it again.

 For more information, see Chapter 10 in *Excel For Dummies, Second Edition.*

Macros: Running a Macro

If you don't assign a keyboard shortcut to a macro or add the macro to the Tools menu, you have to run the macro from the <u>T</u>ools⇨<u>M</u>acro command. Here's the procedure:

1. Invoke the <u>T</u>ools⇨<u>M</u>acro command to summon the Macro dialog box.

2. Select the macro that you want to run from the list of macros currently available.

 3. Click <u>R</u>un.

 For more information, see Chapter 10 in *Excel For Dummies, Second Edition.*

Names: Assigning a Name to a Range

Excel lets you assign meaningful names to individual cells or cell ranges that can make your formulas easier to understand. Here's the procedure for assigning a name to a cell or range of cells:

1. Select the cell or range of cells to which you want to assign a name.

2. Call up the <u>I</u>nsert⇨<u>N</u>ame⇨<u>D</u>efine command to summon the Define Name dialog box.

3. Type a name for the cell or cell range in the Names in <u>W</u>orkbook box.

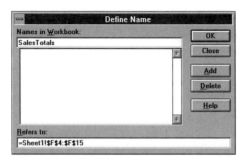

4. Click OK to dismiss the Define Name dialog box.

To use a range name in a formula, type the name anytime you would type a range. For example, instead of =**Sum(F4:F15)**, use the formula =**Sum(SalesTotals)**.

To delete a range name, call up the Insert⇨Name⇨Define command, select the range name that you want to delete, and click Delete.

You can quickly select a named range by pressing F5 to call up the Go To dialog box (or use the Edit⇨Go To command) and double-clicking the range name in the list box.

For more information, see Chapter 5 in *Excel For Dummies,* Second Edition.

Notes: Adding a Note to a Cell

Excel lets you add an electronic version of those yellow sticky notes to your worksheets. Just follow these steps:

1. Click the cell to which you want to add the note.

2. Call up the Insert⇨Note command or press Shift+F2.

3. Type anything you want in the Text Note box.

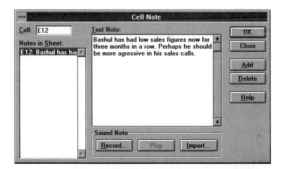

4. Click OK.

A blue dot is added to the cell to indicate that a note is attached to it. To call up the note later, click the cell and press Shift+F2 or choose the Insert➪Note command.

To delete a note, call up the Insert➪Note command to display the note and then click Delete.

After you call up the Cell Note dialog box, you can peruse other notes by selecting them in the Notes in Sheet list box.

For more information, see Chapter 5 in *Excel For Dummies,* Second Edition.

Replace: Replacing Data

You can use the Edit➪Replace command to replace all occurrences of one bit of text with some other text. Here's the procedure:

1. Press Ctrl+Home to move to the top of the worksheet. If you skip this step, the search-and-replace operation starts at the current cell.

2. Choose Edit➪Replace or press Ctrl+H to summon the Replace dialog box:

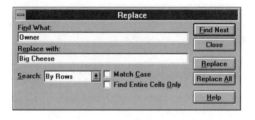

3. Type the text that you want to find in the Find What field; type the text that you want to replace the Find What text in the Replace With field.

4. Click the Find Next button. When Excel finds the text, it moves the cell pointer to the cell that contains the text.

5. Click Replace to replace the text.

6. Repeat the Find Next and Replace sequence until you're finished.

You can change the direction of the search by changing the setting for the Search drop-down box. The choices are

- **By Rows:** Searches all the cells of one row before moving on to the next row.

- **By Columns:** Searches all the cells of one column before moving on to the next column.

Check the Match Case option before beginning the search if it matters whether the text appears in uppercase or lowercase letters.

If you want to find text only if the entire cell entry matches the Find What text, check the Find Entire Cells Only option.

You can use the following wildcard characters in the Find What text:

- **?** finds a single occurrence of any character. For example, **f?t** finds *fat* or *fit.*

- ***** finds any combination of characters. For example, **b*t** finds any combination of characters that begins with *b* and ends with *t,* such as *bat, bait, ballast,* and *bacteriologist.*

If you're absolutely positive that you want to replace all occurrences of the Find What text with the Replace With text, click Replace All. This step automatically replaces all remaining occurrences of the text. Using the Replace All feature may be a problem because you're bound to encounter at least one instance in which you don't want the replacement to occur. Replacing the word *mit* with *glove,* for example, changes Smith to Sgloveh (and no, *Sgloveh* is not the Czechoslovakian form of the name *Smith*).

For more information, see Chapter 5 of *Excel For Dummies,* Second Edition.

Styles: Applying a Style

You can apply the style to any other cell or range of cells by following these steps:

1. Select the cell or cells you want to format.

2. Choose the Format➪Style command.

3. Select the style from the Style Name list.

4. Click OK.

If you find yourself working with styles regularly, you may want to add a Style control to one of the toolbars. Call up the View➪Toolbars command and then click the Customize button. Select Formatting in the Categories list and then drag the Style button out of the Customize dialog box and onto one of the toolbars.

For more information, see Chapter 3 in *Excel For Dummies,* Second Edition.

Styles: Creating a Style

A *style* is a collection of formatting attributes that you can apply
to a cell or range of cells all at the same time. It's a bit of a hassle
to go to the trouble of setting up a style, but if you find yourself
frequently applying the same combination of formats, it's worth
it. Here's the procedure for creating a style:

1. Toil over a cell until you get it formatted exactly the way
   you want.

2. Choose Format⇨Style.

3. In the Style Name field, type the name of the style that you
   want to create. Then check off the formatting attributes that
   you want to include in the style:

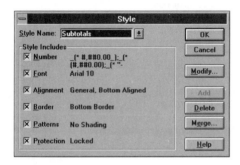

4. Click OK.

Note that you don't have to include all the formatting attributes in
a style. For example, if you create a style that includes just the
Font, Border, and Patterns attributes, only those attributes are
changed when you apply the style to a cell.

Part IV

PowerPoint

This part covers PowerPoint, the desktop presentation program that comes with Microsoft Office. PowerPoint is like Word in many respects, except that it's geared toward producing *presentations* rather than *documents*.

In PowerPoint lingo, a presentation consists of a sequence of *slides*. After you create the slides, you can print them on plain paper or on transparencies for overhead projection, or you can have them made into glorious 35mm color slides. You can print handouts with two, three, or six slides on each page, notes pages to help you bluff your way through your presentation, and a complete outline of your presentation.

The PowerPoint Screen

The following figure shows what PowerPoint's screen looks like when you're editing a presentation.

In the center of the screen is the main presentation window. In this example, only one presentation is open, and its window is maximized so that it fills all the space available within the main PowerPoint window. However, you can open more than one presentation file and display the files at the same time in separately sizable windows.

Along the left edge of the presentation window is the Drawing toolbar, which contains buttons that let you effortlessly add text or graphic objects to your slides.

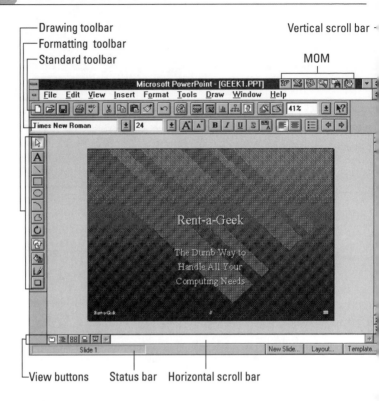

Drawing toolbar

Formatting toolbar

Standard toolbar

Vertical scroll bar

MOM

View buttons   Status bar   Horizontal scroll bar

The status bar at the bottom of the screen provides helpful information about the presentation. Also notice the vertical scroll bar at the right edge of the screen and the horizontal scroll bar just above the status bar, which allow you to navigate through your presentation. To the left of the horizontal scroll bar are several buttons that let you switch among the different types of views available in PowerPoint.

The double-headed arrow buttons at the bottom of the vertical scroll bar allow you to move forward or backward through your presentation one slide at a time.

The Standard toolbar contains a variety of buttons that perform common functions. Just click a button to perform the function. To find out what each button does, hold the mouse pointer over the button for a moment. A bright yellow tool tip appears, indicating the button's function. The Formatting toolbar lets you quickly apply the most common formats, including style, font, size, bold, italic, underline, alignment, numbered and bulleted lists, and indentation.

By clicking one of the view buttons next to the horizontal ruler, you can quickly switch to a different view. The three buttons on the status bar provide quick shortcuts for common operations. Click the New Slide button in the status bar to create a new slide, the Layout button to change the layout of a slide, or the Template button to assign a different template to the current presentation.

Roll Call of Keyboard Shortcuts

Unlike most other Office programs, PowerPoint is inherently mouse oriented. Nevertheless, you will still find occasions when you'd rather not move your fingers off the keyboard just to apply a simple formatting command or invoke some other PowerPoint feature. Fortunately, just about every imaginable PowerPoint operation has a keyboard shortcut. The following sections describe the most useful shortcuts.

Editing

Shortcut	*What It Does*
Ctrl+X	Cuts selected text to the Clipboard.
Ctrl+C	Copies selected text to the Clipboard.
Ctrl+V	Pastes the contents of the Clipboard.
Ctrl+Z	Undoes the last action.
Ctrl+Delete	Deletes a word (forward).
Ctrl+Backspace	Deletes a word (backward).
Ctrl+F	Finds text.
Ctrl+H	Replaces text.

Changing Views

Shortcut	*What It Does*
Ctrl+Alt+N	Switches to slide view, which shows slides as they appear when printed or displayed.

(continued)

Shortcut	What It Does
Ctrl+Alt+O	Switches to outline view, which shows an outline of your presentation.
Ctrl+Alt+P	Switches to slide sorter view, which shows several slides at once so you can easily rearrange them.

Navigating and Selecting

Shortcut	What It Does
Ctrl+←	Moves the insertion point one word to the left.
Ctrl+→	Moves the insertion point one word to the right.
Ctrl+↑	Moves the insertion point to the preceding paragraph, except in outline view, in which it moves to the preceding slide.
Ctrl+↓	Moves the insertion point to the next paragraph, except in outline view, in which it moves to the next slide.
End	Moves the insertion point to the end of the line.
Home	Moves the insertion point to the beginning of the line.
Ctrl+End	Moves the insertion point to the end of the page.
Ctrl+Home	Moves the insertion point to the top of the page.
Ctrl+Alt+PgUp	Moves to the preceding slide in slide sorter view.
Ctrl+Alt+PgDn	Moves to the next slide in slide sorter view.
Ctrl+A	Selects everything.

Formatting

TIP Although the easiest way to select text is by dragging the mouse, you can also select text by holding down the Shift key while using these keyboard shortcuts.

(continued)

Shortcut	What It Does
Ctrl+B	Makes text **bold**.
Ctrl+I	Sets the font to *italic*.
Ctrl+U	<u>Underlines text (continuous).</u>
Ctrl+Shift+F	Changes the font.
Ctrl+Shift+P	Changes the point size.
Ctrl+Shift+>	Increases the point size to the next available size.
Ctrl+Shift+<	Decreases the point size to the preceding size.
Ctrl+Alt+>	Raises the baseline.
Ctrl+Alt+<	Lowers the baseline.
Ctrl+L	Left-aligns the paragraph.
Ctrl+R	Right-aligns the paragraph.
Ctrl+J	Justifies the paragraph.
Ctrl+E	Centers the paragraph.

Drawing

Shortcut	What It Does
Ctrl+Shift+G	Groups the selected objects.
Ctrl+Shift+H	Ungroups the selected group.
Ctrl+Shift+J	Regroups the grouped object that you just ungrouped.

Inserting Objects

Shortcut	What It Does
Ctrl+M	Inserts a new slide by using the AutoLayout dialog box.
Ctrl+Shift+M	Inserts a new slide without using the AutoLayout dialog box.
Alt+Shift+D	Inserts the date on the Slide Master.
Alt+Shift+T	Inserts the time on the Slide Master.

(continued)

Shortcut	What It Does
Alt+Shift+P	Inserts the page number on the Slide Master.
Ctrl+D	Duplicates the selected objects.
Ctrl+A	Selects all objects.

File Management

Shortcut	What It Does
Ctrl+N	Creates a new file.
Ctrl+O	Opens an existing file.
Ctrl+W	Closes the current file.
Ctrl+S	Saves the current file.
F12	Saves the current file by using a new filename.
Ctrl+P	Prints the current file.
Alt+F4	Exits PowerPoint.
Ctrl+F6	Switches to the next presentation window.
Ctrl+Shift+F6	Switches to the preceding presentation window.

Outlining

Shortcut	What It Does
Alt+Shift+←	Promotes the selected paragraphs.
Alt+Shift+→	Demotes the selected paragraphs.
Alt+Shift+↑	Moves the selected paragraphs up.
Alt+Shift+↓	Moves the selected paragraphs down.
Alt+Shift+A	Collapses or expands all text.
/ (on numeric keypad)	Hides or shows character formatting.

Slide Show

Shortcut	What It Does
Enter, spacebar, →, ↓, PgDn, N	Displays the next slide.

(continued)

Shortcut	What It Does
Backspace, ←, ↑, PgUp, P	Displays the preceding slide.
1+Enter	Displays the first slide.
(Slide number)+Enter	Displays a specific slide.
B, period (.)	Toggles the screen to black.
W, comma (,)	Toggles the screen to white.
A, =	Shows or hides the pointer.
E	Erases screen doodles.
S, +	Stops or restarts automatic show.
H	Displays the next slide, even if it is hidden.
(Slide number), Enter	Displays a specific hidden slide.
Esc, Ctrl+Break, minus (– on numeric keypad)	Ends the slide show.

Best Loved Procedures

The following sections contain a hodge-podge of procedures for working with various aspects of PowerPoint.

Builds: Adding Builds to a Slide

A *build effect* lets you display the bullet paragraphs on a slide one at a time. Each time you press Enter during the slide show, the next bullet paragraph in sequence drops onto the slide. To set up build effects, follow this procedure:

1. Switch to slide sorter view.

2. Click the slide to which you want to add a build effect.

3. Choose the Tools⇨Build command. The Build dialog box appears:

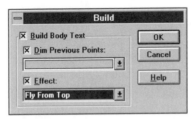

4. Pick a build <u>E</u>ffect from the drop-down list box.

5. Check <u>D</u>im Previous Points if you want the bullet items that have already been displayed to switch to a different color as each new bullet item is displayed. The color is picked from the color scheme, but you can override PowerPoint's choice if you want.

6. Click OK or press Enter.

For more information, see Chapter 10 in *PowerPoint 4 For Windows For Dummies.*

Clipart: Using ClipArt

Here is the procedure for adding clip art to your presentation:

1. Move to the slide that you want to decorate with clip art. (If you want the clip art to appear on every slide, move to the master slide by using the <u>V</u>iew⇨<u>M</u>aster⇨<u>S</u>lide Master command or Shift-clicking the Slide View button.)

2. Choose <u>I</u>nsert⇨<u>C</u>lip Art. The ClipArt Gallery dialog box pops up:

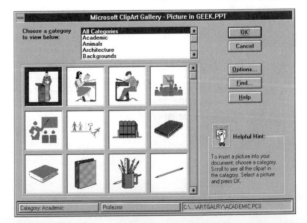

3. Select the category from the list box that contains the picture that you want.

   Note: When you first pop up the ClipArt Gallery, *All Categories* is selected; this category shows all the ClipArt pictures in your collection. To narrow your search, scroll the Category list until you find the category that you want and click it.

4. Select the specific picture you want. ClipArt Gallery shows 12 pictures at a time, but you can display other pictures from the same category by scrolling through the pictures. When the picture you want comes into view, click it.

5. Click OK to insert the picture.

   PowerPoint sticks the picture right in the middle of the slide, which is probably not where you want it. You can move and resize it by dragging it with the mouse.

The first time you use ClipArt Gallery after installing PowerPoint, ClipArt Gallery realizes that it hasn't added PowerPoint's clip art to the gallery, so it automatically adds the clip art. This process can take a while, so be prepared.

For more information, see Chapter 12 in *PowerPoint 4 For Windows For Dummies.*

Color: Changing the Color Scheme

Here is the procedure to follow for changing your presentation's color scheme:

1. Switch to Slide Master view by choosing View⇨Master⇨ Slide Master.

2. Use the Format⇨Slide Color Scheme command to summon the Slide Color Scheme dialog box:

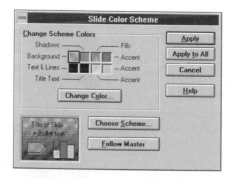

3. Click the Choose Scheme button to open the Choose Scheme dialog box:

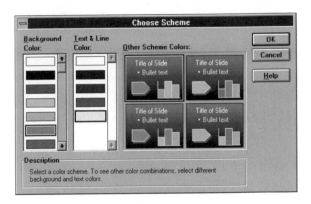

4. Click the Background color you want to use. The Background Color box contains 90 background colors you can choose from; use the scroll bar if the background color you want to use isn't visible.

5. Click one of the Text & Line colors that appear after you select the background color.

6. Select one of the four color schemes that appear after you select the Text & Line color. (If you don't like any of these color schemes, go back and pick another Background or Text & Line color.)

7. Click OK or press Enter to return to the Slide Color Scheme dialog box with your newly chosen color scheme displayed.

8. Click the Apply button to apply the new color scheme to the Slide Master.

For more information, see Chapter 9 in *PowerPoint 4 For Windows For Dummies.*

Find: Finding Text

You can use the Edit⇨Find command to find text anywhere in a presentation. Just follow these steps:

1. Move to the first slide of the presentation. This step is optional, but it usually makes sense to search for text starting from the beginning of the file.

2. Use the Edit⇨Find command or press Ctrl+F to summon the Find dialog box.

3. Type the text you want to find in the Find What field:

4. Click the Find Next button.

5. Wait a second while PowerPoint searches your presentation. When it finds the text, it moves to the slide that contains the text and highlights the text on-screen. The Find dialog box remains on-screen so that you can click Find Next to find yet another occurrence of the text:

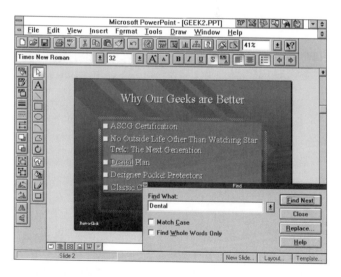

6. When it reaches the end of the presentation, PowerPoint displays the following message:

7. If you started at the beginning of the file, click Cancel and get on with your life. Otherwise, click Continue to resume the search from the beginning of the presentation.

Check the Match Case option before beginning the search if it matters whether the text appears in uppercase or lowercase letters. This option is handy when you have, for example, a presentation about Mr. Smith the Blacksmith.

Use the Match Whole Word Only option to find your text only when it appears as a whole word. If you want to find the text in which you talk about Mr. Smith the Blacksmith's mit, for example, type **mit** in the Find What text and check the Match Whole Word Only option. That way, the Find command looks for *mit* as a separate word. It doesn't show you all the *mit*s in Smith and Blacksmith.

If you find the text you're looking for and decide that you want to replace it with something else, click the Replace button. Then skip ahead to the procedure for replacing text.

For more information, see Chapter 2 in *PowerPoint 4 For Windows For Dummies*.

Master: Adding Recurring Text

To add recurring text to each slide, follow this procedure:

1. Call up the Slide Master if it's not displayed already.

2. Click the Text Tool button in the Drawing toolbar.

3. Click where you want to add text.

4. Type the text that you want to appear on each slide.

5. Format the text however you want.

6. Click the Slide View button to return to slide view.

To add a graphic that recurs on each slide, click the Insert ClipArt button in the Standard toolbar to insert any clip art picture supplied with PowerPoint or use the Insert⇨Picture command to insert a picture file.

To delete an object from the Slide Master, click it and press Delete. To delete a text object, you must first click the object and then click the object frame again. Then press Delete.

If the object won't select when you click on it, you've probably fallen back into slide view. Shift-click the Slide View button or use the View⇨Master⇨Slide Master command again to call up the Slide Master.

For more information, see Chapter 8 in *PowerPoint 4 For Windows For Dummies*.

Master: Hiding Background Objects

Slide Masters let you add background objects that appear on every slide in your presentation. If you want, you can hide these objects for a particular slide by following this procedure:

1. Display the slide you want to show with a plain background.

2. Choose Format⇨Slide Background to summon the Slide Background dialog box:

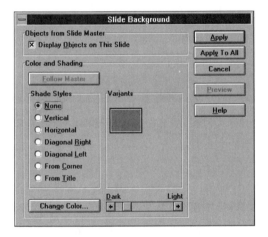

3. Uncheck Display Objects On This Slide.

4. Click the Apply button or press Enter.

This procedure for hiding background objects applies only to the current slide or notes page. Other slides or notes pages are not affected.

You can also hide objects in the background of Notes Pages by performing the procedure just described while working in notes pages view. Instead of the Format⇨Slide Background command, use the Format⇨Notes Background command.

If you want to remove some but not all of the background objects from a single slide, try this trick:

1. Follow the preceding procedure to hide background objects for the slide.

2. Call up the Slide Master (choose View⇨Master⇨Slide Master).

3. Hold down the Shift key and click each object that you want to appear on the slide.

4. Press Ctrl+C to copy these objects to the Clipboard.

5. Return to slide view.

6. Press Ctrl+V to paste the objects from the Clipboard.

7. Use the Draw⇨Send to Back command if the background objects obscure other slide objects or text.

For more information, see Chapter 8 in *PowerPoint 4 For Windows For Dummies.*

Master: Shading the Slide Background

Shading for the slide background works much like the color scheme. When you apply it to the Slide Master, every slide that follows the master picks it up. Alternatively, you can apply it to an individual slide, or you can apply it to all slides without changing the master. Here's the procedure for shading the slide background:

1. To shade the background for the Slide Master (and thus for all slides that follow the master), Shift-click the Slide View button or choose the View⇨Master⇨Slide Master command.

   To shade just one slide, switch to slide view and display the slide that you want to shade. To shade several slides, switch to slide sorter view and hold down the Shift key while clicking the slides that you want to shade.

2. Choose Format⇨Slide Background to call up the Slide Background dialog box.

3. Select the shade style you want (vertical, horizontal, and so on) by clicking one of the Shade Styles buttons.

4. Select the variations for the shade style you want by clicking one of the preview boxes in the Variants area of the Slide Background dialog box.

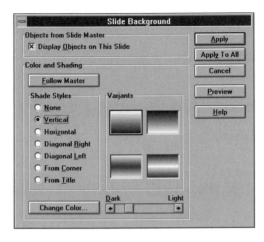

5. Click Apply to apply the shading to just the slide (or slides) that you selected or Apply To All to apply the shading to all slides.

When you apply a template, all background shading specified for the template's masters is applied along with the color scheme.

You can change the color scheme's background color by clicking the Change Color button in the Slide Background dialog box.

For more information, see Chapter 8 in *PowerPoint 4 For Windows For Dummies.*

Notes: Adding Notes to a Slide

To add notes to a slide, follow this procedure:

1. In slide or outline view, move to the slide to which you want to add notes.

2. Switch to notes pages view.

3. Adjust the zoom factor with the Zoom drop-down list in the Stardard toolbar if necessary so you can read the notes text.

4. If necessary, scroll the display to bring the notes text into view.

5. Click the box that reads Click to add text.

6. Type away.

The text you type appears in the notes area. You can use any of PowerPoint's standard word processing features, such as cut, copy, and paste, as you create your notes. Press Enter to create new paragraphs.

After you switch to notes pages view, you don't have to return to slide view or outline view to add notes for other slides. Use the scroll bar or the PgUp and PgDn keys to add notes for other slides.

For more information, see Chapter 4 in *PowerPoint 4 For Windows For Dummies*.

Printing: Printing Slides, Notes Pages, Handouts, and Outlines

Here's the procedure for printing your presentation's slides, notes pages, handouts, or outlines:

1. Choose File➪Print. The Print dialog box appears:

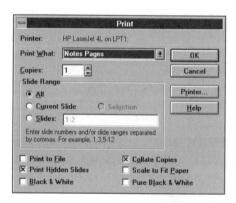

2. Use the Print What list box to select the presentation component you want to print: Slides, Notes Pages, Handouts, or Outline.

3. If you want hidden slides included in the printout, make sure that the Print Hidden Slides box is checked.

4. Click OK or press Enter.

For more information, see Chapter 6 in *PowerPoint 4 For Windows For Dummies*.

Replace: Replacing Text

You can use the Edit➪Replace command to replace all occurrences of one bit of text with some other text. Here's the procedure:

1. Move to the first slide in the presentation. If you skip this step, the search-and-replace operation starts at the insertion point.

2. Use the Edit➪Replace command or press Ctrl+H to summon the Replace dialog box.

3. Type the text that you want to find in the Find What field, and type the text that you want to replace it with in the Replace With field.

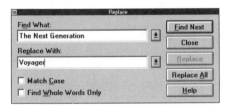

4. Click the Find Next button. When Word finds the text, it highlights it:

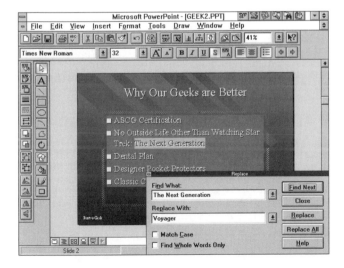

5. Click the <u>R</u>eplace button to replace the text:

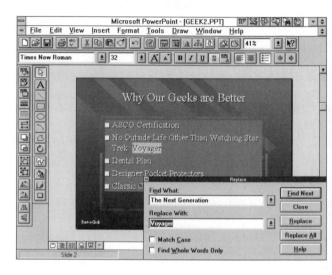

6. Repeat the <u>F</u>ind Next and <u>R</u>eplace sequence until you're finished.

Check the Match <u>C</u>ase option before beginning the search if it matters whether the text appears in uppercase or lowercase letters. This option is handy when you have a presentation about Mr. Smith the Blacksmith, for example.

Use the Match <u>W</u>hole Words Only option to find your text only when the text is whole word. If you want to find the text in which you talk about Mr. Smith the Blacksmith's mit, for example, type **mit** in the Fi<u>n</u>d What text and check the Match <u>W</u>hole Word Only option. That way, the Find command looks for *mit* as a separate word. It doesn't show you all the *mit*s in Smith and Blacksmith.

If you're absolutely positive that you want to replace all occurrences of your Fi<u>n</u>d What text with the Re<u>p</u>lace With text, click the Replace <u>A</u>ll button. This action automatically replaces all remaining occurrences of the text. The only problem is that you're bound to encounter at least one spot where you don't want the replacement to occur. Replacing the word *mit* with *glove,* for example, changes Smith to Sgloveh (and no, *Sgloveh* is not the Czechoslovakian form of the name *Smith*).

For more information, see Chapter 2 in *PowerPoint 4 For Windows For Dummies.*

Slide Show: Adding Transitions

To set the transitions between slides, follow this procedure:

1. Use the <u>V</u>iew⇨Sli<u>d</u>e Sorter command to switch to slide sorter view or click the Slide Sorter button.

2. Select the slide to which you want to add a transition.

3. Choose <u>T</u>ools⇨<u>T</u>ransition. The Transition dialog box appears:

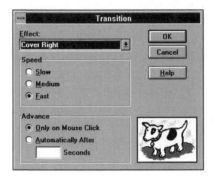

4. Select the transition <u>E</u>ffect you want from the drop-down list box.

5. Select the Speed of the transition. (Fast is almost always best.)

6. Click OK or press Enter.

Slide Show: Viewing Your Slides

Here's the procedure for displaying a slide show:

1. Click the Slide Show View button. The first slide in your presentation appears.

2. To advance to the next slide, press Enter, press the spacebar, or click the left mouse button.

3. Press Esc to end the slide show.

Sorter: Rearranging Slides in Slide Sorter View

One of the easiest ways to quickly rearrange slides is by switching to slide sorter view, in which you can see a thumbnail version of each slide in a presentation. Here's the procedure for rearranging slides in slide sorter view.

1. Switch to slide sorter view by clicking the Slide Sorter View button at the bottom-left corner of the screen or by choosing <u>V</u>iew⇨Sli<u>d</u>e Sorter.

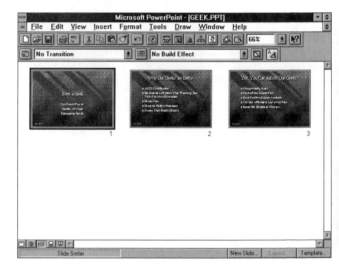

2. To move a slide, click and drag it to a new location. PowerPoint adjusts the display to show the new arrangement of slides.

3. To delete a slide, click the slide and press the Delete key. (The Delete key works on an entire slide only in slide sorter view.) You can also use the <u>E</u>dit⇨Delete Sl<u>i</u>de command.

4. To add a new slide, click the slide that you want the new slide to precede and click the New Slide button. The New Slide dialog box appears so that you can pick the layout for the new slide. To edit the contents of the slide, return to slide or outline view.

If your presentation contains more slides than will fit on-screen at the same time, you can use the scroll bars to scroll the display. Or you can change the zoom factor to make the slides smaller. Click the down arrow next to the zoom size and select a smaller zoom percentage.

For more information, see Chapter 2 in *PowerPoint 4 For Windows For Dummies.*

Sound: Adding a Sound

To add obnoxious noises to your presentations, follow these steps:

1. Move to the slide to which you want to add the sound.

2. Press Alt+Tab until the Windows Program Manager returns to your screen. Find the Sound Recorder icon, which hides in the Program Manager Accessories group.

3. Double-click the Sound Recorder icon to start it. The Sound Recorder dialog box appears:

4. Choose the File⇨Open command to open the sound file that you want to insert. You may have to rummage through your hard disk to find the file. Keep looking; it's there somewhere.

5. Click the Play button to make sure that you found the right sound.

6. Choose Edit⇨Copy to copy the sound to the Clipboard.

7. Hold down Alt and press Tab until you see PowerPoint in the box on-screen. Release both keys, and PowerPoint comes back to life.

8. Use the Edit⇨Paste command to paste the sound. A miniature replica of the Sound Record icon appears to let you know that the sound is there.

9. Double-click the sound icon to hear the sound.

By default, embedded sounds play automatically in a slide show during the transition into the slide that contains the sound or when you click the sound icon. You can change this behavior by selecting the sound in slide view and choosing the Tools⇨Play Settings command. Doing so summons the Play Settings dialog box:

- Check When Click on Object if you want to be able to play the sound at will by clicking its icon.

- Check Hide While not Playing to hide the icon during the slide show (except when the sound is actually playing).

- Check When Transition to have the sound play automatically during the transition into the slide. Also, check Starts to play the sound at the beginning of the transition or Ends to play the sound when the transition ends. Add a time delay if you don't want the sound to play immediately.

 For more information, see Chapter 17 in *PowerPoint 4 For Windows For Dummies*.

Spelling: Spell Checking a Presentation

Here's the procedure for checking a presentation's spelling:

1. If the presentation that you want to check is not already open, open it. It doesn't matter which view you're in. You can spell check from slide, outline, notes pages, or slide sorter view.

2. Click the Spelling button in the Standard toolbar, press F7, or choose Tools⇨Spelling.

3. Wait patiently while PowerPoint searches your presentation for embarrassing spelling errors.

4. If PowerPoint finds a spelling error in your presentation, it switches to the slide that contains the error, highlights the offensive word, and displays the misspelled word along with a suggested correction:

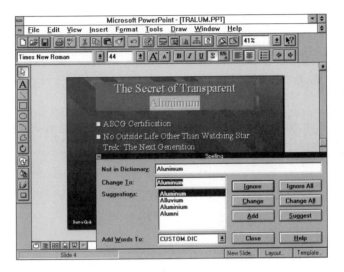

5. If you agree that the word is misspelled, scan the list of corrections that PowerPoint offers and click the one you like. Then click the Change button. If you like the way you spelled the word in the first place (maybe it's an unusual word that isn't in PowerPoint's spelling dictionary, or maybe you like to spell like Chaucer), click the Ignore button. Watch as PowerPoint turns red in the face.

6. You're done when you see the following message:

Note that PowerPoint checks spelling for titles, body text, notes, and text objects added to slides. However, it doesn't check the spelling in embedded objects such as charts or graphs.

TIP If PowerPoint can't come up with a suggestion, or if none of its suggestions is right, you can type your own correction and click the <u>C</u>hange button. If the word you type isn't in the dictionary, PowerPoint asks you whether you're sure that you know what you're doing. Double-check and click OK if you really mean it.

If you want PowerPoint to ignore all occurrences of a particular misspelling, click the I<u>g</u>nore All button. Likewise, if you want PowerPoint to correct all occurrences of a particular misspelling, click the Change <u>A</u>ll button.

For more information, see Chapter 5 in *PowerPoint 4 For Windows For Dummies*.

Tabs: Setting Tabs and Indentation

To set tab stops and indents, follow these steps:

1. Switch to slide view. You can't change tabs or indents in outline view.

2. Activate the ruler by using the <u>V</u>iew⇨<u>R</u>uler command.

3. Select the text object whose tabs or indents you want to change.

Indentation doohickey   Ruler

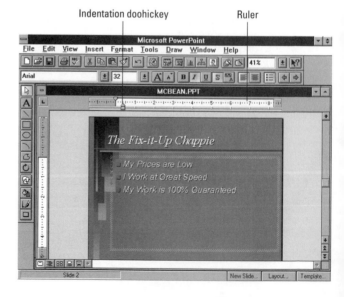

4. Click the ruler to add a tab stop.

5. Grab the indentation doohickey and drag it to change the indentation.

Each text object has its own tab settings. The tab settings for an object apply to all paragraphs within the object, so you can't change tab settings for individual paragraphs within a text object.

In PowerPoint's outline view, you use the Tab key to demote text to the next lower outline level. The Ctrl+Tab command performs the traditional tabbing function. To advance text to the next tab stop, press Ctrl+Tab.

To remove a tab stop, use the mouse to drag it off the ruler.

For more information, see Chapter 7 in *PowerPoint 4 For Windows For Dummies.*

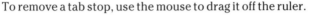

Viewer: Using the PowerPoint Viewer

Suppose you have a desktop computer with umpteen hundreds of megabytes of disk storage on which you can create your presentations, but you need to show the presentation on a laptop computer that's almost out of free disk space. No problem! All you have to do is install the PowerPoint Viewer program on the laptop and copy the PowerPoint presentation files (PPT extension) to the laptop. You don't need the entire PowerPoint program just to run a slide show.

Here's the procedure for displaying a slide show by using the Viewer:

PowerPoint
Viewer

1. Start PowerPoint Viewer by double-clicking its icon, which should be hiding in the Microsoft Office Program Manager groups.

2. Select the presentation you want to show from the Viewer dialog box.

3. Click Show.

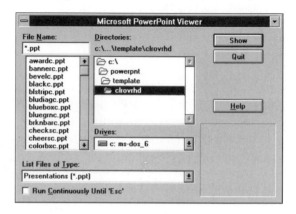

 If you use a desktop computer to create PowerPoint presentations and a laptop or notebook computer to run them, you don't
have to install the full PowerPoint program on the laptop or
notebook computer; just install the Viewer.

 If you want to set up a computer to run a slide show over and
over, click Run Continuously Until 'Esc'. For a truly unattended
presentation (like at a trade show), be sure to hide the keyboard
and mouse or unplug them from the computer after you get the
slide show going. Leaving a keyboard unattended is like inviting
all the computer geeks within five miles to step up to your
computer and find out which games you have.

 Make sure that the computer on which you run the slide show
has all the fonts that the presentation requires. If it doesn't, or if
you're not sure, use the File⇨Save As command to save the file
and then check the Embed TrueType Fonts button. Doing so
stores a copy of the fonts used by the presentation in the
presentation file.

 For more information, see Chapter 10 in *PowerPoint 4 For Windows
For Dummies.*

Part V

Access

This part covers Access, the database program that comes with Microsoft Office Professional. Access isn't included in Office Standard Edition, so you can skip this part if you don't have Office Professional.

Access is a powerful database program that computer programmers can use to create sophisticated applications. On the other hand, it is simple enough that novice computers can put it to use (well, perhaps after a wee bit of practice).

The Access Screen

The following figure shows what the Access screen looks like after you open a database.

In the center of the screen is the main database window. As you can see, it contains several buttons and tabs that you use to work with databases.

The title bar at the very top of the Access window works the same as the title bar in any Windows program. The buttons labeled MOM are actually displayed by Microsoft Office Manager running in small icon mode. If you don't have MOM or don't use it, these buttons won't appear on your computer.

You can call up a special control menu by clicking the application control box, or you can quickly quit Access by double-clicking this box. You can also use the Minimize and Maximize buttons to alter the size of the window.

The menu bar in Access constantly changes. Each time you switch to a different type of database object, Access adds or removes menu items. Many Windows programs do this to some degree, but Access does it more than probably every other program you've ever used.

The Database toolbar contains a variety of buttons that perform frequently used functions. In every other Office program, this toolbar is called the Standard toolbar. Access calls it the Database toolbar just to be different.

Click a button to perform the function. To find out what each button does, hold the mouse over the button for a moment. A bright yellow tool tip appears, indicating the button's function.

The database window represents all the objects that comprise a single database file. These objects are organized into six groups, as indicated by the notebook-style tabs that run down the left edge of the window: tables, queries, forms, reports, macros, and modules. To select one of these groupings, just click the tab.

At the top of the database window are three buttons. The New button creates a new object of whatever type is currently selected. To open an existing object, click the object and then click Open. To redesign an existing object, click the object and then click Design. Clicking any of these three buttons causes Access to open a new window to hold the object.

As you work with Access, various bits of interesting information about the database makes its way to the status bar at the bottom of the screen. In this example, however, there's not much of interest to see.

Roll Call of Keyboard Shortcuts

Like most of the other Office programs, Access has more keyboard shortcuts than you could possibly remember. Here is a sampling of the best feats of Access prestidigitation.

General Editing

Shortcut	What It Does
Ctrl+X	Cuts text to the Clipboard.
Ctrl+C	Copies text to the Clipboard.
Ctrl+V	Pastes text from the Clipboard.
Ctrl+Z	Undoes the last action.
Esc	Undoes changes to the current field or record.
Ctrl+F	Finds text.
Ctrl+H	Replaces text.
Ctrl+A	Selects all records.

Working with Datasheets

Shortcut	What It Does
F2	Switches between editing a field and navigating the datasheet.
F5+(record number)	Goes to a specific record.
Tab, Enter, or →	Goes to the next field.
Shift+Tab or ←	Goes to the preceding field.
Home	Goes to the first field in the current record.
End	Goes to the last field in the current record.

(continued)

Shortcut	What It Does
Ctrl+Home	Goes to the first field in the first record.
Ctrl+End	Goes to the last field in the last record.
Ctrl+↑	Goes to the current field in the first record.
Ctrl+↓	Goes to the current field in the last record.
PgDn	Moves down one screen.
PgUp	Moves up one screen.
Ctrl+PgDn	Moves right one screen.
Ctrl+PgUp	Moves left one screen.

Working with Forms

Shortcut	What It Does
F2	Switches between editing a field and navigating the datasheet.
F5+(record number)	Goes to a specific record.
Tab, Enter, or →	Goes to the next field.
Shift+Tab or ←	Goes to the preceding field.
Home	Goes to the first field in the current record.
End	Goes to the last field in the current record.
Ctrl+Home	Goes to the first field in the first record.
Ctrl+End	Goes to the last field in the last record.
Ctrl+↑	Moves to the current field in the first record.
Ctrl+↓	Moves to the current field in the last record.
Ctrl+PgDn	Moves to the current field in the next record.

(continued)

Shortcut	What It Does
Ctrl+PgUp	Moves to the current field in the preceding record.
Ctrl+Tab	Leaves subform and returns to the next field in the main form.
Ctrl+Shift+Tab	Leaves the subform and returns to the preceding field in the main form.
Ctrl+Shift+Home	Leaves the subform and returns to the first field in the main form.

Data Entry Shortcuts

Shortcut	What It Does
Ctrl+;	Inserts the current date.
Ctrl+Shift+:	Inserts the current time.
Ctrl+Alt+Spacebar	Inserts the field's default value.
Ctrl+' or Ctrl+Shift+"	Inserts the field's value from the preceding record.
Ctrl+Shift++ (plus sign)	Adds a record.
Ctrl+– (minus sign)	Deletes the current record.
Ctrl+Enter	Inserts a new line in a field, label, or expression zoom box.
Shift+Enter	Saves changes to the current record.

File Menu Shortcuts

Shortcut	What It Does
Ctrl+N	Creates a new database.
Ctrl+O	Opens an existing database.
Ctrl+S	Saves a file.
F12	Saves a file under a new name or in a new format.
Ctrl+P	Prints a file.
Alt+F4	Exits the program.
Ctrl+F6	Goes to the next database window.

Best Loved Procedures

The following sections contain some basic procedures for working with Access. These procedures represent the most basic functions you're apt to use Access for: creating a new database and a table, adding fields to a table, creating a query to extract specific information from the database, and creating and printing reports. Access is considerably more complex than the other Office programs, as you can tell from the number of steps required even for these basic procedures.

Creating a New Database

The most basic of all Access procedures — and the one you'll want to use as soon as you grow bored of playing with the sample databases — is creating a new database. Here is the step-by-step procedure:

1. Start Access by clicking the Access button in Microsoft Office Manager or by double-clicking the Access icon in Program Manager.

2. Click the New button or use the File⇨New Database command. The New Database dialog box appears:

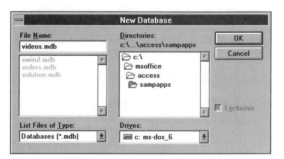

3. Type the name of the database you want to create. In the preceding example, I typed **VIDEOS.MDB** as the filename.

4. Click OK. Access whirs and spins for a moment, and then an empty database window appears:

5. You now have created a database, but it has nothing in it. To create a table within the database, click the New button in the database window. The New Table dialog box appears:

6. Click the Table Wizards button to call up the Table Wizard. Access grinds and churns for a moment, and then the Table Wizard makes its appearance:

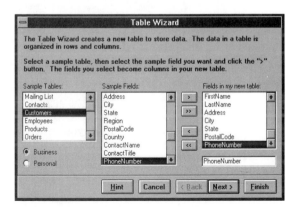

7. Access provides 45 sample tables you can use as a starting point for your table — 26 for business use and 19 for personal use. Pick the one that seems like it best describes the table you want to create by clicking it in the Sample Tables list. (To switch from business to personal tables, click the Personal button beneath the list.) In this example, I picked the Customers sample table.

8. The fields that are in the Sample Tables appear in the Sample Fields list. Copy the fields you want to include in your table by selecting the sample field and then clicking the > button.

9. To include all the Sample Fields in your table, click the >> button.

10. After you add all the fields you want to include in your table, click the Next > button. The next screen of the Table Wizard appears:

11. If you don't like the name Access picks for your table, type a new name. Then click Next >. The last Table Wizard screen appears:

Finish

12. If you want Access to create a form for you so you can enter data, click the third option button. Then click the Finish button. Access buzzes and hums for a few moments. Then the form appears:

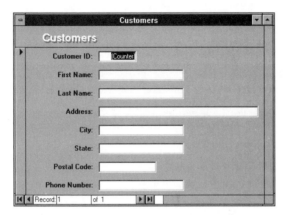

13. Now you can enter data into the form. Use the Enter or Tab key to move from field to field. After you enter the data for the last field on the form (in the preceding example, Phone Number), press Enter to enter the record into the table and call up a new blank form for the next record.

14. When you're finished entering data, double-click the control box at the top-left corner of the form. Access asks whether you want to save changes to the form. Note that the data you've entered into the table has already been saved; this question asks whether you want to save the form design that the Table Wizard automatically created. Click Yes. The Save As dialog box appears:

15. Type a name for the form (in this example, I typed **Customers**) and then click OK to save the form.

Whew! That's enough for now.

After you become proficient with Access, you may want to forego the Table Wizard and design your own tables from scratch. However, even experienced Access users can save time by using the Table Wizard to copy fields from the sample tables.

If you want to add additional fields to the table after you finish with the Table Wizard, use the "Adding a Field to an Existing Table" procedure, described next.

The Table Wizard allows you to mix and match fields from various sample tables. After you copy fields from one sample table, pick a different one from the Sample Tables list and continue to copy fields.

Adding a Field to an Existing Table

After you have defined a table, it's a simple matter to add additional fields. The following procedure creates a new field by using a field in one of the sample tables as a model:

 1. From the Database window, click the Table tab, click the table to which you want to add a field, and then click the Design button. The table design window appears:

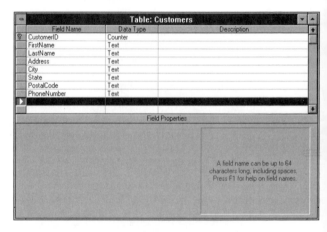

2. Click the row in which you want to insert the new field. To insert the new field after the existing fields, click the first blank row.

3. Click the Build button. The Field Builder dialog box appears.

4. Select the sample table that contains the field you want to add from the Sample Tables list and then select the field from the Sample Fields list.

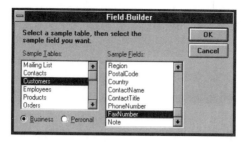

5. Click OK. The field is added to the table:

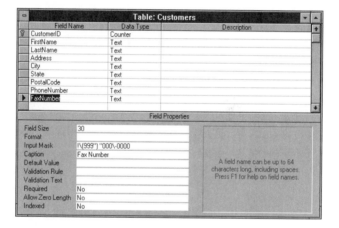

6. Double-click the control box at the upper-left corner of the table design window. When asked whether you want to save changes to the table design, click Yes.

If you prefer to define the field manually, or if no similar field is in any of the sample databases, skip steps 3–5. Instead, follow this procedure:

1. From the Database window, click the Table tab, click the table to which you want to add a field, and then click the <u>D</u>esign button. The table design window appears.

2. To insert the new field after the existing fields, click the first blank row.

3. To insert the new field among the existing fields, click where you want to insert the new field and then click the Insert Row button.

4. Type the name of the new field in the Field Name column.

5. Select the field type from the drop-down list in the Data Type column. (The down arrow that activates the drop-down list appears when you move the insertion point to the Data Type column. Click the arrow to show the list of field types.)

6. A list of field properties specific to the type of field you selected appears at the bottom of the Table Design dialog box. Adjust the properties however you see fit.

7. Double-click the control box at the upper-left corner of the table design window. When asked whether you want to save changes to the table design, click Yes.

Creating a Query

A query is the most powerful and difficult-to-use feature of Access. Before you create a query, you need to know the following details:

• Which tables are involved in the query

• Which fields you want the query result to show

• What sequence you want the query result sorted into

• Which criteria you want to apply to determine which records are selected

Here is the blow-by-blow procedure for creating a query:

1. Open the database for which you want to create a query. Click the Query tab in the Database window and then click the New button. The New Query dialog box appears:

2. Click the New Query button. I know you're tempted to use the Wizard, but it's designed to help you create more complicated queries. For simple queries, use the New Query button. Access displays the query window and the Add Table dialog box.

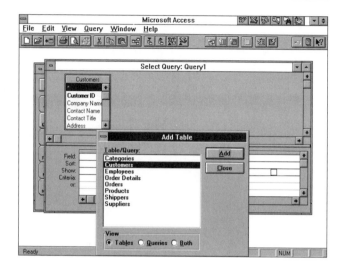

3. Double-click each table you want to include in the query. In the preceding example, I added just one table to the query window. After you add all the tables you need, click Close.

4. Double-click each field you want to include in the query to add it to a column in the bottom part of the query window. If you want the query result to be sorted, select the sort fields first. Here's what the query window looks like after several fields have been selected:

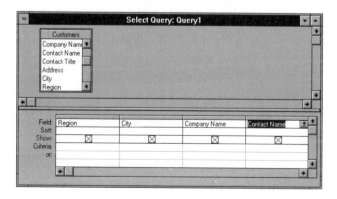

5. Select the sort order for the query result by clicking in the sort row for each field by which you want the result sorted, clicking the drop-down arrow to reveal the list of sort choices, and selecting Ascending or Descending sort

sequence from the list. Do this for each field by which you want the query result sorted. In the following example, the query result is sorted first by Region and then by City:

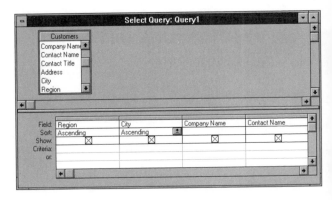

6. Type the query selection criteria in the Criteria rows for the fields whose values you want to test. In the following example, the Region field is tested so that only those records whose Region field is 'OR' or 'WA' are included in the query result.

7. Click the Run button to run the query. The query results are displayed in a separate window:

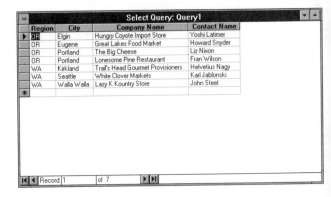

8. If the query works as expected, use the File⇨Save command to save it. The Save As dialog box appears.

9. Type a meaningful name for the query and then click OK.

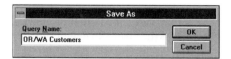
Save As

Query **Name:**

OR/WA Customers

OK

Cancel

After you save the query, you can run it at any time by calling up the Database window, clicking the Query tab, and double-clicking the query name in the list of queries.

When you type the criteria, you can use any of the following comparison symbols:

Symbol	Meaning
=	Equal to
<	Less than
>	Greater than
<=	Less than or equal to
>=	Greater than or equal to
<>	Not equal to

You can also specify a range of values by using Between . . . and, as in *Between 10 and 50.*

Creating a Report

Access has a very powerful set of Report Wizards that automatically create various types of reports after asking you questions about the information you want to include. Follow these steps to create a simple tabular report, which prints a simple listing of database records with one record per line and the fields neatly lined up in columns. The procedure for creating other types of reports is similar.

1. Open the database for which you want to create a report. Click the Report tab in the Database window and then click the New button. The New Report dialog box appears:

New Report

Select A **Table/Query:**

Customers

Report **Wizards**   **Blank Report**

Cancel

2. Click the Report Wizards button. This action summons the Report Wizards dialog box, which displays a list of the various wizards that are available:

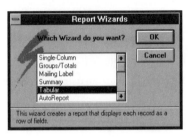

3. Click Tabular to select the Tabular Report Wizard and then click OK. The Tabular Report Wizard appears:

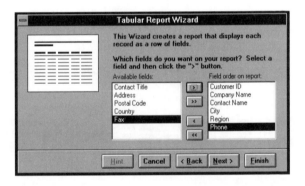

4. Select the fields you want to include in the report by clicking each field and then clicking the > button. Each field you select is removed from the Available fields list and inserted in the Field order on report list.

5. After you select all the fields you want to include, click the Next > button. The Tabular Report Wizard dialog box asks its next question.

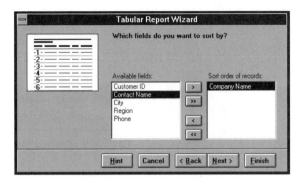

6. Select the fields by which you want to sort the report, once again by clicking each field and then clicking the > button. In this example, I told the Wizard to sort the report into Company Name sequence.

7. After you select all the fields by which you want to sort the report, click the Next > button. The Tabular Report Wizard dialog box asks yet another question:

8. Pick the report style that suits your fancy (the report preview under the big magnifying glass changes as you select different report styles). Then click Next >. The Tabular Report Wizard dialog box asks its final question.

9. Change the report title if you don't like the one that the Wizard proposes, and then click the Finish button. The Wizard grinds and churns for a few moments while it creates the report and then displays it in preview mode:

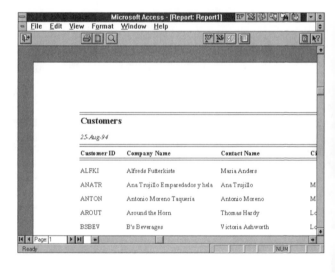

 10. To print the report, click the Print button.

11. To save your report design, choose File⇨Save. Access asks you for a report name.

12. Type a report name and then click OK to save the report.

Part VI

Mail

This part covers Mail, the electronic-mail program that doesn't come with Microsoft Office.

Wait a minute. If Mail doesn't come with Office, why do I include a chapter about it in this book? Because although Office doesn't include a copy of Mail, it comes with the next best thing: a piece of paper that legally entitles you to copy the Mail software from a network server onto your computer, assuming that your computer is hooked up to a network and the network mavens at your company have purchased the Mail program to run on the network.

The Mail Screen

The following figure shows what Mail's screen looks like.

In the center of the screen is the main window you work with when using Mail, called the *Inbox*. The Inbox lists the headers of all messages that other users have sent to you. You can read a message by double-clicking its icon.

Mail has a second window called the *Outbox* that you work with occasionally. The Outbox holds messages that you send to other users until the messages can be delivered.

The toolbar contains a variety of buttons that perform frequently used functions. As you can see, Mail uses larger buttons than the other Office programs. And the toolbar isn't customizable: what you see is what you get.

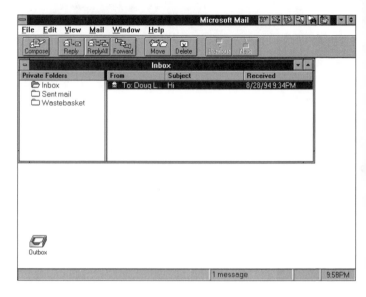

Click a toolbar button to perform the function. Also, the tool-tip feature that pops up a yellow box describing a button's function when you allow the pointer to hover over the button for a moment doesn't work in Mail. Too bad.

The status bar tells you how many messages are in your Inbox and how many of them haven't been read yet. In addition, a cute little picture of a letter coming in through the mail slot appears when you have unread mail.

Roll Call of Keyboard Shortcuts

Mail has a number of keyboard shortcuts that can simplify your everyday e-mail chores.

Command Shortcuts

Shortcut	Equivalent Command
Ctrl+A	<u>M</u>ail⇨Reply to <u>A</u>ll

Shortcut	Equivalent Command
Ctrl+C	Edit⇨Copy
Ctrl+D	File⇨Delete
Ctrl+F	Mail⇨Forward
Ctrl+G	View⇨Open Inbox
Ctrl+M	File⇨Move
Ctrl+N	Mail⇨Compose Note
Ctrl+P	File⇨Print
Ctrl+R	Mail⇨Reply
Ctrl+T	View⇨Toolbar
Ctrl+V	Edit⇨Paste
Ctrl+X	Edit⇨Cut
Ctrl+Z	Edit⇨Undo

Editing Messages

Shortcut	What It Does
Tab	Moves to the body of the message.
Shift+Tab	Moves to the message heading.
Ctrl+←	Moves one word left.
Ctrl+→	Moves one word right.
Ctrl+Home	Moves to start of the message.
Ctrl+End	Moves to end of the messsage.

Working with the Address Book

Shortcut	What It Does
Ctrl+A	Adds a name to the Personal Address Book.
Ctrl+F	Finds a name.
Ctrl+L	Opens a directory.
Ctrl+N	Creates a new address.
Ctrl+P	Opens the Personal Address Book.

E-Mail Abbreviations

E-mail nerds also like to use shorthand abbreviations for common words and phrases, such as FYI (For Your Information) and ASAP (As Soon As Possible). Sometimes these abbreviations can be hard to figure out for the uninitiated. Here are some common abbreviations:

Abbreviation	*What It Means*
BTW	By the Way
FWIW	For What It's Worth
IMO	In My Opinion
IMHO	In My Humble Opinion
IOW	In Other Words
ROFL	Rolling on the Floor, Laughing
ROFL,PP	Rolling on the Floor, Laughing, Peeing My Pants
TIA	Thanks in Advance
TTFN	Ta Ta for Now (à la Tigger)
TTYL	Talk to You Later
<g>	Grin
<bg>	Big Grin

Smileys

E-mail doesn't have the advantage of voice inflections, the absence of which can lead to all sorts of misunderstandings. Therefore, be careful to let people know when you are joking and when you really mean what you say. E-mail nerds have developed a peculiar way to convey tone of voice: they string together symbols on the computer keyboard to create *smileys*. The following table lists the most commonly used (and abused) smileys.

Smiley	*What It Means*
:-)	Just kidding.
;-)	Wink.
:-(	Bummer.
:-0	Well, I never!
:-x	My lips are sealed.

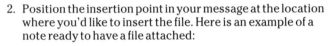

Best Loved Procedures

Attaching a File to a Message

To attach a file to an e-mail message, follow these steps:

1. Follow the "Composing and Sending a Message From Mail" procedure through step 8.

2. Position the insertion point in your message at the location where you'd like to insert the file. Here is an example of a note ready to have a file attached:

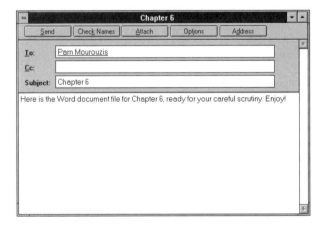

3. Click the <u>A</u>ttach button. The Attach dialog box appears.

4. Select the file you want to attach and then click the <u>A</u>ttach button. The next figure shows how the Attach dialog box looks after you have selected the file:

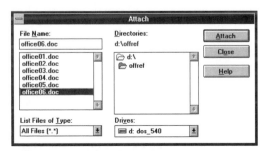

5. If necessary, repeat step 4 to attach additional files.

6. Click Close after you have attached all the files you want. With a Word document attached to your message, your message should look something like this:

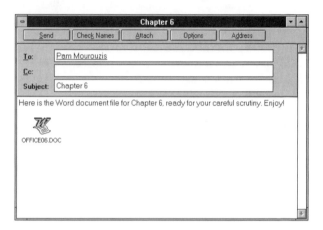

7. Click the Send button to send the message.

Composing and Sending a Message from Mail

Here is the procedure for composing and sending an e-mail note from Mail:

1. From Mail, click the Compose button. The Send Note dialog box appears, as shown in the following figure.

2. Click the Address button to call up the Address list, as shown in the second figure.

3. Click the name of the person to whom you want to send the note and then click the To button. The name is copied to the To list.

4. Repeat step 3 if you want to send the message to more than one person.

5. If you want a copy of the note sent to another person, click the person's name and then click the Cc button. The name is copied to the Cc list.

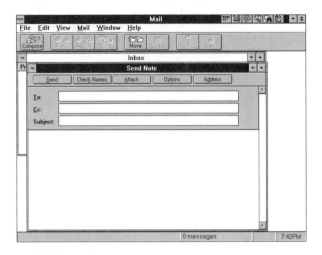

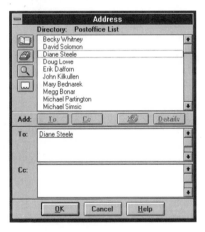

6. Click OK when the address is complete. You return to the Send Note dialog box.

7. Type the message subject in the Subject text field.

8. Type the text of your message in the message area. The following figure illustrates a completed message that is ready to send.

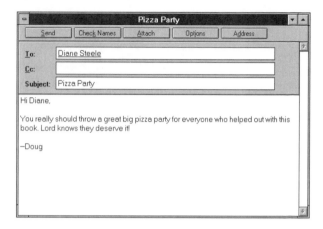

9. Click the Send button to send the message.

Creating a Personal Mail Group

A *personal mail group* is a list of names that you can use to distribute Mail messages. Personal mail groups are an easy way to distribute e-mail to everyone who is involved with a project. After you set up the group, any mail that you send to the group name is automatically sent to everyone in the group.

Here is the procedure for creating a personal mail group:

1. Call up the Mail⇨Personal Groups command. The Personal Groups dialog box appears:

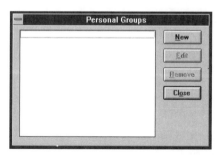

2. Click the New button to create a new group. The New Group dialog box appears.

3. Type a name for the group you want to create.

4. Click the Create button. Yet another dialog box appears, this one listing all the names available in your mail directory.

5. Double-click each name that you want to include in the group. The following figure shows the group looks like after several names have been added:

6. Click OK after you've added everyone to the group. The original Personal Groups dialog box is displayed with the new group listed.

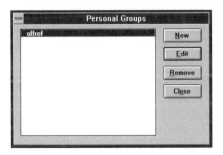

7. Click the Close button to dismiss the Personal Groups dialog box.

Reading a Message

If Mail is running on your computer when a message arrives from someone else on the network, a beep lets you know (unless you or someone else has disabled the beep option by using the Mail⇨Options command or your computer doesn't have sound capability) and an envelope flashes on-screen (unless this option is also disabled). When you have mail waiting, you can read it by following these steps:

1. In Mail, make sure that the Inbox window is displayed.

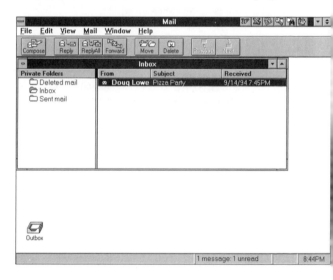

2. Double-click the envelope icon of the message you want to read. The message opens.

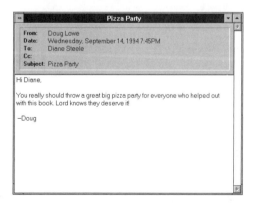

3. If the message contains an attached file, double-click the file's icon to display the contents of the file.

4. After you read the message, you can dispose of it in any of the following ways:

   • Click the Delete button to delete the message.

   • Click the Reply button to reply to the message. See the procedure "Replying to a Message" later in this part for details.

   • Click the Forward button to forward the message to another user. You must supply the name of the person you want the message forwarded to, and you have the option of adding your own comments to the message.

   • Choose the File⇔Print command to print the message.

Replying to a Message

To reply to a message, follow these steps:

1. Open and read the message by following the "Receiving a Message" procedure.

2. Click the Reply button. A dialog box in which you can compose your reply appears. Notice that the subject is automatically set to indicate the message you are replying to, and the original message appears in the reply so that the recipient of your reply knows what you're talking about.

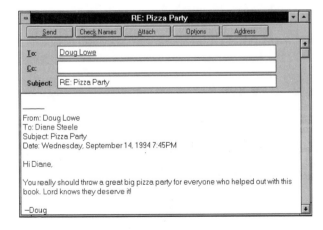

3. Type your reply.

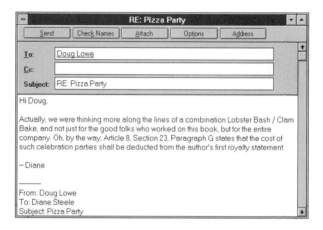

4. Click the Send button to send your reply.

Routing a Document to Several People

The Routing Slip feature lets you send a document from Word, Excel, or PowerPoint to several people in sequence. When you set up a routing slip and send the document, the document is sent to the first person listed in the routing list. When that person receives the document, he or she can review and edit the file and then forward it to the next person on the list, who in turn reviews and edits the document and forwards it to the next person, and so on until the end of the list is reached. If you want, you can place your own name at the end of the list so the document is returned to you after everyone has had a chance to review it.

Sending a document with a routing list

Here's the procedure for sending a document with a routing list:

1. In Word, Excel, or PowerPoint, open the document that you want to route and then choose File⇨Add Routing Slip. The Routing Slip dialog box appears.

2. Click the Address button to summon the Address dialog box.

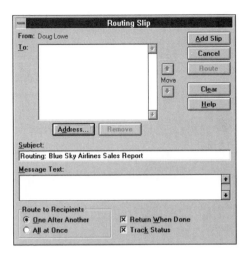

3. For each person you want to include in the Routing Slip, click the person's name and then click the Add button. The names are copied to the To list.

4. Click the OK button to return to the Routing Slip dialog box.

5. Click the Route button to send the document to the first person on the routing slip.

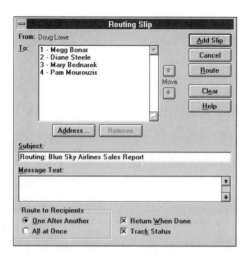

Receiving and forwarding a routed document

If you are unfortunate enough to be included in a document's routing list, you receive a Mail note similar to the following example when the document comes your way.

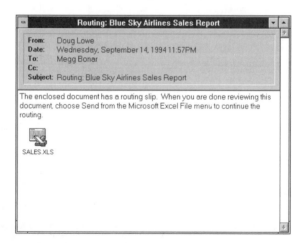

Follow these steps to review or edit the document and send it on to the next person on the list:

1. Double-click the icon in the routing note. The application that created the document (Word, Excel, or PowerPoint) opens the document.

2. Review and edit the document.

3. When you're ready to send the document to the next person on the list, choose File⇨Send. The following dialog box appears.

4. Click the OK button to route the document to the next poor soul.

Sending Mail from an Office Application

You can send a file to another user directly from Word, Excel, or PowerPoint by using the File⇨Send command. Using this command has the same effect as composing a message in Mail and attaching the document file to the message but spares you the drudgery of using Mail directly. Here's the procedure:

1. In Word, Excel, or PowerPoint, open the file you want to send and then choose File⇨Send. The Send Note dialog box appears. Here's how it looks when invoked from Word:

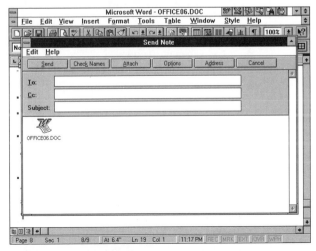

The icon in the note indicates that the document file has been attached.

2. Click the Address button to call up the Address list.

3. Click the name of the person you want to send the file to and then click the To button. The name is copied to the To list.

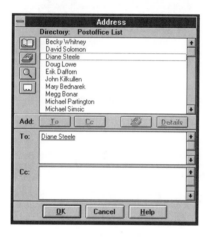

4. Repeat step 3 if you want to send the file to more than one person.

5. If you want to send a copy of the file to a user, click the user's name and then click the Cc button. The name is copied to the Cc list.

6. Click OK when the address is complete. You return to the Send Note dialog box.

7. Type the subject in the Subject text field.

8. Type a message if you wish. The next figure shows how a note looks when it's ready to send.

9. Click the Send button to send the file.

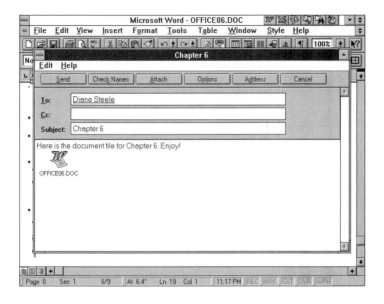

Part VII

Office Applet Programs

In addition to Word, Excel, PowerPoint, Mail, and Access, Microsoft Office comes with several smaller programs called *Applets.* These Applet programs can create fancy pictures, or *objects,* that you can imbed within other Office programs. You can call up the Applet program used to create the picture at any time simply by double-clicking the object.

Office includes the following Applet programs:

- **Microsoft ClipArt Gallery:** Inserts clip art pictures.
- **Microsoft Equation Editor:** Creates Einstein-like equations.
- **Microsoft Graph:** Creates spectacular-looking graphs and charts.
- **Microsoft OrgChart:** Creates organization charts so you know who reports to whom.
- **Microsoft Picture:** Draws pictures.
- **Microsoft WordArt:** Creates fancy logos.

The following sections summarize the toolbar buttons, keyboard shortcuts, and common procedures for each Applet program.

Microsoft WordArt

Microsoft WordArt is specially designed for formatting text in strange ways. You usually use it to create logos.

WordArt is an OLE 2 program, which means that when you run WordArt, it takes over the window that was formerly occupied by Word, PowerPoint, or whatever program was running. Here's what Microsoft Word looks like after WordArt takes it over:

WordArt Buttons

When you work in WordArt, WordArt's toolbar replaces whatever toolbar was visible in the program from which you called WordArt. Here's the lowdown on the buttons and gizmos that are available from WordArt's toolbar:

Button	What It Does
— Plain Text	Lets you select one of 36 basic shapes. WordArt folds, spindles, and mutilates your text to make it fit the shape you select.
Arial	Sets the text font.
10	Sets the font size. Usually, you should leave this set to Best Fit to allow WordArt to pick an appropriate font size.
B	Makes the text **bold**.
I	Makes the text *italic*.
Ee	Makes all characters the same height, whether they are uppercase or lowercase.

(continued)

Button	What It Does
◁	Flips letters on their sides.
⬛	Stretches the text to fill the selected shape.
⬛	Displays a window of alignment choices (Center, Left, Right, plus three types of justification).
⬛	Displays a dialog box that enables you to adjust spacing.
⬛	Displays a dialog box that enables you to rotate the text.
⬛	Selects a pattern or color for the text.
⬛	Selects one of several shadow types for the text.
⬛	Adjusts the thickness of the text outline.

Inserting a WordArt Object

The following procedure works with Word, Excel, and PowerPoint.

1. Position the insertion point where you want to insert the WordArt object. In Word or PowerPoint, just click the mouse pointer to mark the location. In Excel, highlight the range of cells into which you want to insert the WordArt.

2. Choose Insert⇨Object. When the Object dialog box appears, select Microsoft WordArt 2.0 as the Object Type:

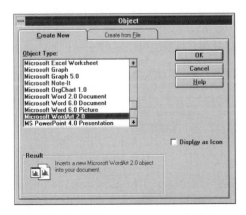

3. Click OK. WordArt springs to life, replacing Word's, Excel's, or PowerPoint's menus and toolbars with its own:

4. Type some text in the Enter Your Text Here box and then click the Update Display button to transfer the text you typed to the WordArt object on-screen.

5. Click the Shape tool to reveal a menu of shapes that you can use to contour your text:

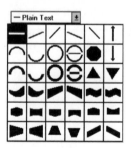

6. Click the shape in the shape list. The text is reshaped to fit the shape you selected, as the following figure shows.

7. Fool around with the other WordArt controls on the toolbar. (The function of each control is described earlier in this section.) WordArt looks like the second figure after you apply a shadow by using the Shadow button and change the text color by using the Shading button.

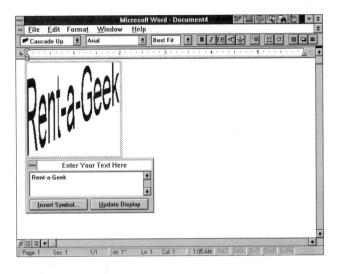

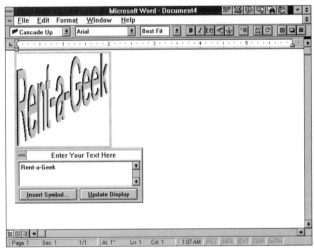

8. Click anywhere outside the WordArt object frame to return to the program from which you called WordArt. The WordArt object remains in the document and Word's, Excel's, or PowerPoint's regular menus and toolbars return to view.

The procedure for inserting a WordArt object in Access is similar, but you use the Edit⇨Insert Object command instead of the Insert⇨Object command.

Microsoft Graph

Microsoft Graph 5 is a charting program that can create pie charts, bar charts, line charts, and just about any other type of chart imaginable. Graph is intended to be used from Word, PowerPoint, or Access. A charting feature similar to Graph is built into Excel.

Like WordArt, Graph is an OLE 2 program. When you call it up, it takes over the menus and toolbars of the program from which you call it. Here's what Graph looks like from Word:

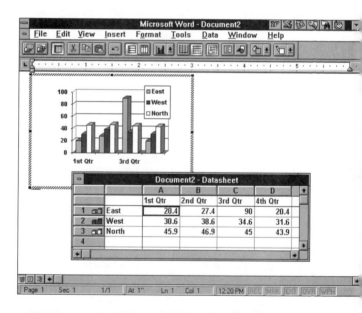

Graph Toolbars

Graph comes with three different toolbars that you can activate via the View⇨Toolbars command.

The Standard toolbar

Button	What It Does
	Imports data into the datasheet.
	Imports a chart.
	Shows the datasheet window.
	Cuts the selection to the Clipboard.
	Copies the selection to the Clipboard.
	Pastes the contents of the Clipboard.
	Undoes the most recent action.
	Plots data series by datasheet rows.
	Plots data series by datasheet columns.
	Changes the chart type.
	Adds vertical gridlines.
	Adds horizontal gridlines.
	Adds a legend.
	Adds a text box.
	Shows or hides the Drawing toolbar.
	Applies a color to the selection.
	Applies a pattern to the selection.

The Drawing toolbar

Button	What It Does
	Draws a straight line.
	Draws an arrow.
	Draws a squiggly line.
	Draws a rectangle. To make a perfect square, hold down Shift while you draw.
	Draws a circle or oval. Hold down Shift while you draw to create a perfect circle.
	Draws an arc (not the kind Noah used, but a curved line). Hold down Shift while you draw to create a perfect quarter-circle arc.

(continued)

Button	What It Does
	Draws a freeform shape.
	Draws a filled rectangle. To make a perfect square, hold down Shift while you draw.
	Draws a filled circle or oval. Hold down Shift while you draw to create a perfect circle.
	Draws a filled arc. Hold down Shift while you draw to create a perfect quarter-circle arc.
	Draws a filled freeform shape.
	Draws a text box.
	Activates the selection pointer, which makes it easy to select drawn objects.
	Allows you to reshape an object.
	Combines selected objects into a group that behaves as if it were a single object.
	Breaks up a group of objects.
	Brings an object to the front of other objects.
	Sends an object behind other objects.
	Adds a shadow to a drawn object or a range of cells.

The Formatting toolbar

Button	What It Does
Arial	Assigns a font to the selected text.
10	Assigns a point size to the selected text.
B	Applies bold formatting to the selected text.
I	Applies italic formatting to the selected text.
U	Underlines the selected text.
	Left-aligns the paragraph.
	Centers the paragraph.
	Right-aligns the paragraph.

(continued)

Button	What It Does
[$]	Formats the selected cells using the Currency style.
[%]	Formats the selected cells using the Percent style.
[,]	Formats the selected cells using the Comma style.
[.00→]	Increases the number of decimal places for the selected cells.
[→.00]	Decreases the number of decimal places for the selected cells.

Inserting a Graph Object

 You can use the Chart Wizard to create a chart in Excel. A detailed procedure for using the Chart Wizard can be found in Part III of this book.

To create a Microsoft Graph object, follow this procedure:

1. Insert a Graph object by using one of the following methods, depending on the program you're using:

   • **Word:** Click the Insert Chart button or use the Insert⇨Object command and select Microsoft Graph 5.0 as the Object Type.

   • **PowerPoint:** Click the Insert Graph button or choose the Insert⇨Microsoft Graph command. (Alternatively, you can insert a new slide that contains a graph object by clicking the New Slide button in the status bar and selecting a slide type that includes a chart object.)

   • **Excel:** Call up the Insert⇨Object command and select Microsoft Graph 5.0 as the Object Type. Or click the Chart Wizard button in the Standard toolbar and drag the rectangle on the worksheet to indicate where you want the chart inserted. Then follow the instructions in the Chart Wizard. (You can find a step-by-step procedure for using the Chart Wizard in Part III of this book.)

   • **Access:** Call up the Edit⇨Insert Object command and then select Microsoft Graph 5.0 as the Object Type. (You can also create a graph in Access by using the Graph Wizard. Click the Graph tool in the Toolbox and then click where you want to place the graph. Then follow the Graph Wizard's instructions to create your graph.)

Whichever method you use, Microsoft Graph comes to life. It displays its own menus and toolbars and displays a graph and datasheet, using sample data to get you started.

2. Type your own data in the Datasheet window to replace the sample data that Graph provides.

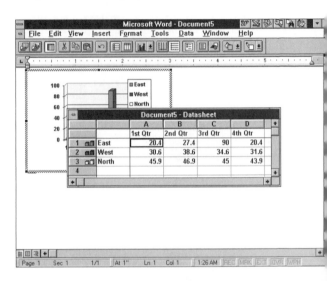

3. Click anywhere outside the chart to return to the program from which you called Graph. The Graph object remains in the document and Word's, Excel's, or PowerPoint's regular menus and toolbars return to view:

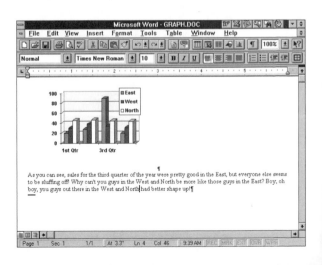

Formatting a Graph

Microsoft Graph has many commands and toolbar buttons that allow you to tweak the appearance of your graph. But the easiest way to improve a graph's appearance quickly is to use one of Graph's AutoFormats. An *AutoFormat* is a combination of a chart type and other graph elements, such as legends, labels, fonts, and colors. Think of AutoFormats as templates for graphs.

Here is the procedure for applying an AutoFormat:

1. Double-click the graph to edit it. Microsoft Graph 5 comes to life, taking over the menus and toolbars.

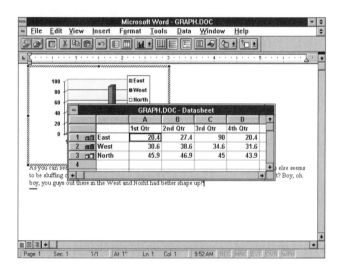

2. Call up the Format⇨AutoFormat command. The AutoFormat dialog box appears.

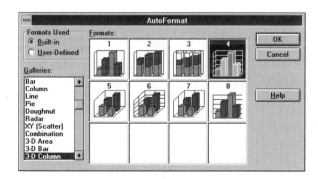

3. Select the chart type you want to use from the Galleries list and then select the specific chart format you want from the Formats shown for the selected chart type. For example, the AutoFormat dialog box appears as shown in the following figure after you select a basic Column chart.

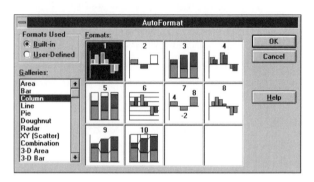

4. Click the OK button to dismiss the AutoFormat dialog box.

5. Click anywhere outside the chart to return to the program from which you called Graph. The Graph object remains in the document and Word's, Excel's, or PowerPoint's regular menus and toolbars return to view.

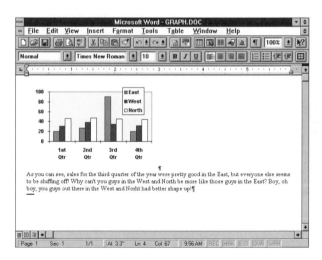

Microsoft Equation Editor

Equation Editor is a special version of a NASA-style equation editor program called MathType, created by Design Science. It is meant to be used with Word or PowerPoint but can be used with Excel and Access as well (assuming that you can find a reason for including a diagram of a complex math equation in Excel or Access, which seems unlikely).

Equation Editor is an OLE 2 program that takes over the calling program's menus and toolbars. When you call it from PowerPoint, it looks like this:

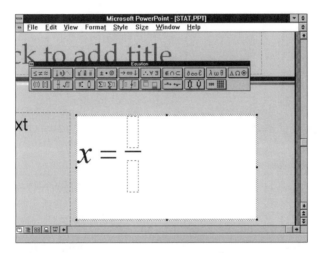

Equation Editor Buttons

Equation Editor probably qualifies for having the nerdiest toolbar of all the Office programs. Though it has but one toolbar, that toolbar includes two types of buttons. The buttons in the top row of the toolbar insert symbols; the buttons in the bottom row insert templates, which are arrangements of cells that can contain equation text.

Symbol buttons

Button	What It Accesses
≤≠≈	Greater-than and less-than signs and similar symbols
⊥ab∴	Spaces in various sizes, plus a few random dots
√ẍ x̄	Cool top hats and things of that sort
±•⊗	A collection of operators that aren't found on the keyboard (+ and – are)
→⇔↓	Various and sundry arrows
∴∀∃	Logical operators
∉∩⊂	Symbols for set theory
∂∞ℓ	Miscellaneous symbols (as if they aren't all miscellaneous!)
λ ω θ	Greek letters
Δ Ω ⊛	More Greek letters

Template buttons

Button	What It Accesses
(⫿) [⫿]	Big parentheses, brackets, braces, and the like
▯/▯ √▯	Templates for creating fractions and roots (like radical, man)
▯▯ ▯̇	Templates with little boxes above or below for superscripts or subscripts
Σ▯ Σ▯▯	Summation templates for using that big Greek Fraternity Sigma thing
∫▯ ∮▯	Integral templates (I knew I should have paid more attention in that Calculus class)
▔▯ ▯▁	Templates with bars above or below
→̇ ←̇	Arrows with templates for text above or below them
Ů Ů	Templates for working with sets
▦ ▦	Matrices of templates

Roll Call of Keyboard Shortcuts

Equation Editor has a number of convenient keyboard shortcuts. Here are the most important ones:

Navigating and Editing Keys

Keyboard Shortcut	What It Does
Tab	Moves to the end of the current slot; if the insertion point is already at the end of the slot, moves to the beginning of the next slot.
Shift+Tab	Moves to the end of the preceding slot.
Ctrl+Tab	Inserts a tab character.
Ctrl+D	Redraws the equation.
Ctrl+Y	Selects all.
Ctrl+Shift+L	Left-aligns.
Ctrl+Shift+C	Centers.
Ctrl+Shift+R	Right-aligns.

Applying Styles

Keyboard Shortcut	What It Does
Ctrl+Shift+=	Applies Math style.
Ctrl+Shift+E	Applies Text style.
Ctrl+Shift+F	Applies Function style.
Ctrl+Shift+I	Applies Variable style.
Ctrl+Shift+G	Applies Greek style.
Ctrl+Shift+B	Applies Matrix-Vector style.

Inserting Symbols

Keyboard Shortcut	What It Inserts
Ctrl+K, I	Infinity (∞)
Ctrl+K, A	Arrow ($\rightarrow$)

(continued)

Keyboard Shortcut	*What It Inserts*
Ctrl+K, D	Derivative ( )
Ctrl+K, <	Less than or equal to ( )
Ctrl+K, >	Greater than or equal to ( )
Ctrl+K, T	Times ($\times$)
Ctrl+K, E	Element of ($\in$)
Ctrl+K, Shift+E	Not an element of ($\notin$)
Ctrl+K, C	Contained in ($\subset$)
Ctrl+K, Shift+C	Not contained in ($\subseteq$)

Inserting Templates

Keyboard Shortcut	*What It Inserts*
Ctrl+9 or Ctrl+0	Parentheses
Ctrl+[or Ctrl+]	Brackets
Ctrl+Shift+{ or Ctrl+Shift+}	Braces
Ctrl+F	Fraction
Ctrl+/	Slash fraction
Ctrl+H	Superscript (high)
Ctrl+L	Subscript (low)
Ctrl+J	Joint superscript/subscript
Ctrl+I	Integral
Ctrl+T, |	Absolute value
Ctrl+R	Root
Ctrl+T, n	nth root
Ctrl+T, S	Summation
Ctrl+T, P	Product
Ctrl+T, M	Matrix
Ctrl+T, U	Underscript (limit)

Inserting an Equation

The following procedure works with Word, Excel, or PowerPoint.

1. Position the insertion point where you want to insert the Equation. Here's an example from Word:

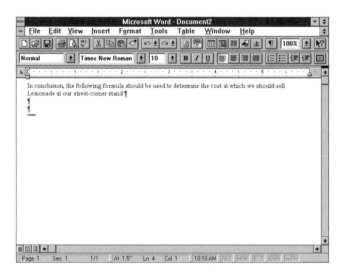

2. Call up the Insert➪Object command (in Access, use the Edit➪Insert Object command). The Object dialog box appears (this dialog box looks slightly different in Excel or PowerPoint).

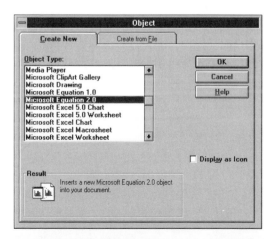

3. Choose Microsoft Equation 2.0 from the Object Type list box and then click OK. Equation Editor takes over, displaying its own menu and a floating toolbar with buttons you use to create the equation.

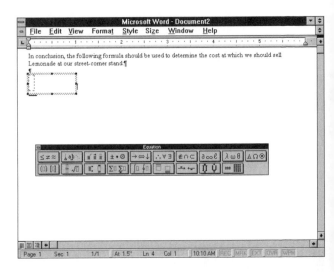

4. Start typing your equation.

5. To add a symbol that's not on the keyboard, use one of the buttons in the top row of the Equation toolbar.

6. To add a stacked symbol, use one of the buttons in the bottom row of the toolbar.

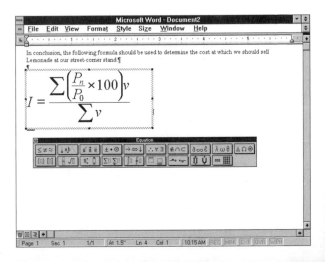

7. When you're done, click anywhere outside the equation. Equation Editor leaves gracefully, returning you to your program.

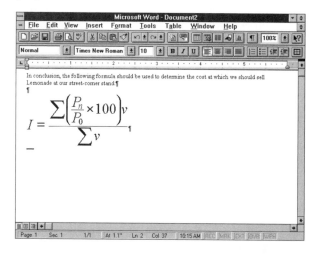

Microsoft OrgChart

Microsoft OrgChart is a slick little program that creates organization charts, such as those used to document corporate structure or federal bureaucracy. It is meant to be used with PowerPoint, but once it's installed, you can use it from any program that has an Insert⇨Object command.

Unlike the other Applets covered so far, OrgChart is *not* an OLE 2 application. When you insert or edit an OrgChart object, OrgChart does not take over the menus and button bars of the host application. Instead, OrgChart opens up its own window in which to work. Here's what OrgChart looks like:

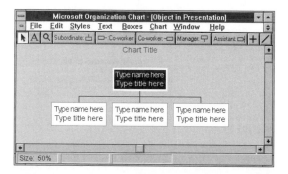

OrgChart's Buttons

OrgChart offers a series of buttons in the toolbar that assist you in drawing your chart.

Button	What It Does
[▶]	Allows you to select chart objects.
[A]	Allows you to enter text into boxes or the chart title area.
[⬜]	Reduces the chart view so that you can see the entire chart.
Subordinate: ⬜	Inserts a new box subordinate to the box you click.
⬜:Co-worker	Inserts a coworker to the left of the box you click.
Co-worker: ⬜	Inserts a coworker to the right of the box you click.
Manager: ⬜	Inserts a manager box above the box you click.
Assistant: ⬜	Inserts an assistant box for the box you click.
[+]	Draws perpendicular lines.
[╱]	Draws a line.
[⋰]	Draws connecting lines.
[□]	Draws a rectangle.
[Q]	Enlarges the chart view so that you can focus on one section of the chart.

Roll Call of Keyboard Shortcuts

OrgChart offers a number of useful keyboard shortcuts for those who are allergic to mouse dander.

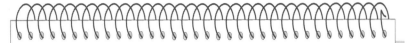

Inserting Boxes

Keyboard Shortcut	What It Does
F2	Inserts a new box subordinate to the box you click.
F3	Inserts a coworker to the left of the box you click.
F4	Inserts a coworker to the right of the box you click.
F5	Inserts a manager box above the box you click.
F6	Inserts an assistant box for the box you click.

Selecting Boxes

Keyboard Shortcut	What It Does
Ctrl+G	Selects all the current box's coworkers (the boxes in the same group).
Ctrl+B	Selects an entire branch, beginning with the current box.
Ctrl+A	Selects all boxes in the chart.
Ctrl+←	Selects the box to the left of the current box.
Ctrl+→	Selects the box to the right of the current box.
Ctrl+↑	Selects the current box's manager.
Ctrl+↓	Selects the first box that reports to the current box.

Inserting an Organization Chart

Follow these steps to create an organization chart:

1. Position the insertion point where you want the organization chart inserted. The following figure shows an example in Word.

2. Call up the Insert⇨Object command (in Access, use the Edit⇨Insert Object command). The Object dialog box appears (this dialog box looks slightly different in Excel or PowerPoint).

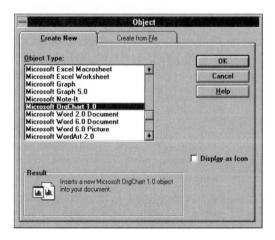

3. Choose Microsoft OrgChart 1.0 from the Object Type list box and then click OK. OrgChart appears in its own window.

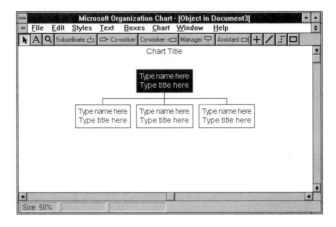

4. Click each box in the organization chart and then type a new name, title, and any other information you want to appear in the chart.

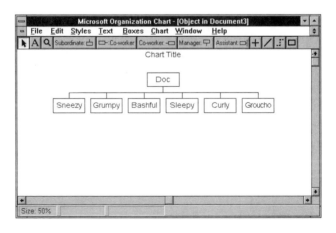

5. To add a new box to the chart, click the Subordinate button and then click the box to which you want the new box to be subordinate. Then type a new name, title, and other information for the box.

Here is what an organization chart looks like when completed:

6. Use the File⇨Exit and Return command to return to your program. A dialog box similar to this one appears:

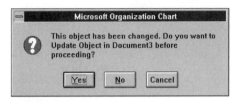

7. Click the Yes button. You return to your document with the organization chart in place.

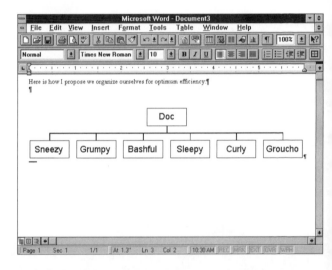

Microsoft ClipArt Gallery

Microsoft ClipArt Gallery is a nifty little program that organizes your clip art files and lets you see the clip art before you insert it into a document. ClipArt Gallery organizes your clip art files into categories, such as Architecture, Flags, and Gestures.

Unlike the other Applets, ClipArt Gallery doesn't use menus, toolbars, or keyboard shortcuts. Instead, ClipArt Gallery uses this dialog box:

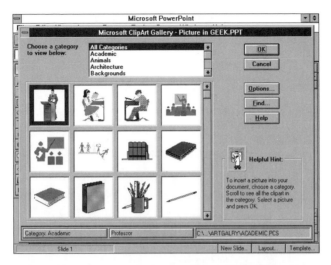

Inserting a ClipArt Gallery Object

To insert a ClipArt Gallery object, follow these steps:

1. Position the insertion point where you want the clip art inserted.

2. Call up the Insert⇨Object command (in Access, use the Edit⇨Insert Object command). The Object dialog box appears (this dialog box looks slightly different in Excel or PowerPoint):

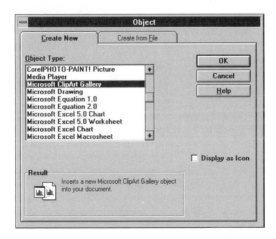

3. Choose Microsoft ClipArt Gallery from the Object Type list box and then click OK. The ClipArt Gallery appears:

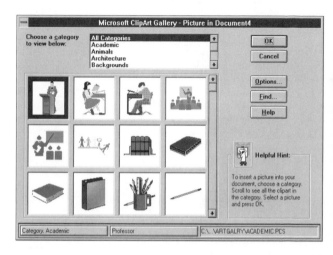

4. Select the category that contains the picture you want from the category list and then select the picture you want to copy into your document. For example, ClipArt Gallery appears as follows after you select a picture from the Cartoons category:

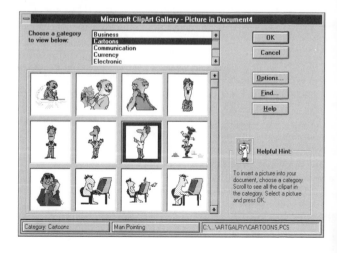

5. Click the OK button. The picture is inserted into your document.

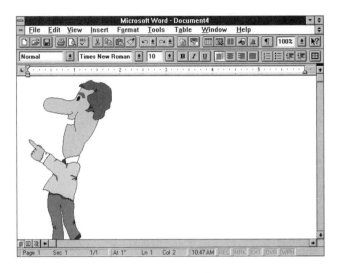

In PowerPoint, you can call up ClipArt Gallery by clicking the Insert Clip Art button in the Standard toolbar. Or you can insert a new slide that contains clip art by clicking the New Slide button in the status bar and selecting a slide type that includes a clip art object.

Part VIII

Working Together

To paraphrase an old cliché, no computer program is an island. The moment you put the final touches on that projected income worksheet, you can bet your bottom dollar that your boss will ask you to give a ten-minute presentation about it at tomorrow's stockholders' meeting and expect a ten-page written report on income trends by the end of the week. Suddenly, you may wish that you had some way to incorporate the Excel worksheet into a PowerPoint presentation and then convert the entire presentation into a Word document.

This part describes various techniques and procedures that let you use the programs that come with Office together. These procedures sometimes go under the $2 buzzword *integration,* and if this weren't a... *For Dummies* book, this part would probably be titled "Integration" instead of "Working Together."

Switching between Programs

One of the best features of Windows is that it lets you run several programs at the same time and switch among them. Using this feature, you can start up Word, PowerPoint, and Excel at the same time and quickly switch to any of the three programs to access or exchange information.

TIP

The number of programs you can run at the same time depends largely on the amount of RAM your computer has. If your computer has but 4MB of RAM, you can probably run two or maybe three programs at the same time, but doing so is kind of like cramming a family of eight into a tiny one-bedroom apartment. With 8MB or more of RAM, running several programs at the same time is a more doable proposition.

After you have several programs running simultaneously, you can switch between them in several ways:

- *Ctrl+Esc*

    You can press Ctrl+Esc at any time to pop up the *task list*, which lists all active programs:

    Find the program you want to switch to in the task list and double-click it.

- *Alt+Esc*

    Press Alt+Esc to switch to the next program in line. If more than two programs are running, you may have to use this key combination several times to get to the program you want.

    You can reverse the order in which Office switches to programs by pressing Alt+Shift+Esc instead.

- *Alt+Tab*

  Alt+Tab displays the name of the most recent program you used:

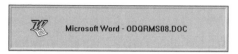

  You can keep pressing the Tab key while holding down the Alt key until the name of the program you want appears. Release both keys to switch to that program.

  You can reverse the order in which Office switches to programs by pressing Alt+Shift+Tab instead.

- *MOM*

  You can switch directly to any Office program by clicking its icon in the Microsoft Office toolbar:

  This technique is most useful when you've configured Microsoft Office to display small icons at the top of the screen, where they appear within the title bar of any maximized application.

Using the Clipboard

Cutting and pasting data via the Clipboard is one of the most basic editing techniques in all the Office programs. It is often the easiest way to share data between programs. The following sections describe how to copy and move data by using the Clipboard.

Copying Data

To copy data from one program to another, follow this procedure:

1. Switch to the program that contains the data you want to copy. If the program isn't already running, start it by switching to Program Manager and double-clicking its icon. If the file that contains the data isn't already open, open it.

2. Highlight the data you want to copy by using the mouse or keyboard.

3. Press Ctrl+C or click the Copy button, which appears in the Standard toolbar of all the Office programs.

4. Switch to the program into which you want to copy the data. If the program isn't already running, start it by switching to Program Manager and double-clicking its icon. If the file you want the data copied into isn't already open, open it.

5. Position the insertion point where you want the data to be inserted.

6. Press Ctrl+V or click the Paste button, which appears in the Standard toolbar of all the Office programs.

Moving Data

To move data from one program to another, follow this procedure:

1. Switch to the program that contains the data you want to move. If the program isn't already running, start it by switching to Program Manager and double-clicking its icon. If the file that contains the data isn't already open, open it.

2. Highlight the data you want to move by using the mouse or keyboard.

3. Press Ctrl+X or click the Cut button, which appears in the Standard toolbar of all the Office programs.

4. Switch to the program into which you want to move the data. If the program isn't already running, start it by switching to Program Manager and double-clicking its icon. If the file into which you want the data copied isn't already open, open it.

5. Position the insertion point where you want the data to be inserted.

 6. Press Ctrl+V or click the Paste button, which appears in the Standard toolbar of all the Office programs.

Linking

Copying data from one program to another is easy enough, but what happens if the data needs to be changed? If you simply copy the data, you must track down every file you copy the data to and update the data in each file. But if you *link* the data, any changes that you make to the original version of the data automatically apply to copies of the linked data.

Linking Data

To copy data from one program to another and create a link, follow this procedure:

1. Switch to the program that contains the data you want to copy. If the program isn't already running, start it by switching to Program Manager and double-clicking its icon. If the file that contains the data isn't already open, open it.

2. Highlight the data you want to copy by using the mouse or keyboard.

 3. Press Ctrl+C or click the Copy button, which appears in the Standard toolbar of all the Office programs.

4. Switch to the program into which you want to copy the data. If the program isn't already running, start it by switching to Program Manager and double-clicking its icon. If the file into which you want the data copied isn't already open, open it.

5. Position the insertion point where you want the data to be inserted.

6. Call up the Edit⇨Paste Special command to summon the Paste Special dialog box:

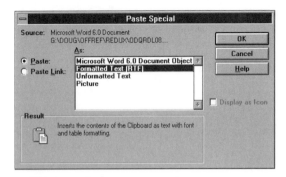

7. Choose the Paste Link option.

8. Click OK.

Whenever you open the file that contains the link, the program checks to see whether the data has changed. If so, it updates the link.

Linking a Document to a File

To insert an entire file into a document and establish a link, follow these steps:

1. In the program and document into which you want the file copied, position the insertion point where you want the file to be inserted.

2. Call up the Insert⇔File command to summon the File dialog box.

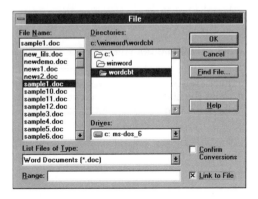

3. Select the file you want to insert. You may have to rummage about the disk a bit to locate the file.

4. Choose the <u>L</u>ink to File option.

5. Click OK.

Breaking a Link

If you grow tired of the link and want to break it, follow this procedure:

1. Switch to the program and file that contain the link. If the program isn't already running, start it by switching to Program Manager and double-clicking its icon. If the file isn't already open, open it.

2. Call up the <u>E</u>dit⇨Lin<u>k</u>s command. The Links dialog box appears:

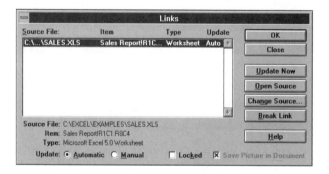

3. Select the link that you want to break.

4. Click <u>B</u>reak Link.

5. When asked whether you really want to break the link, click Yes.

6. If there are still links remaining in the document, click OK to dismiss the Links dialog box. (If you break the last link, the Links dialog box automatically vanishes.)

OLE!

Object Linking and Embedding, or *OLE* for short, is another way to share information between Office programs. When you use OLE, data *objects* are *embedded* into documents. When you double-click an embedded object, you summon the program that originally created the object so that you can edit the object. For example, you can embed a portion of Excel worksheet as an object in a Word document. The worksheet looks pretty much like a Word table when printed, but when you double-click it from within Word, Excel takes over and allows you to edit the table by using all of Excel's spreadsheet editing features. When you're done editing the worksheet, click outside the worksheet object to close Excel and return to Word.

Office supports an advanced form of OLE called OLE 2, which makes the whole process of editing and embedding objects almost transparent. With OLE 1 (also known as OLE Classic), a separate window opens when you edit an embedded object. With OLE 2, the embedded object is edited within the same window as the rest of the document. The program that "owns" the object momentarily takes over the window, supplying its own menus, buttons, and status bar. Most Office programs use the more advanced form of OLE 2 editing, although some of the Applets that I describe in Part VII still use OLE Classic.

Pasting an OLE Object

To paste an OLE object via the Clipboard, follow this procedure:

1. Switch to the program that contains the data you want to embed as an object. If the program isn't already running, start it by switching to Program Manager and double-clicking its icon. If the file that contains the data isn't already open, open it.

2. Highlight the data that you want to embed by using the mouse or keyboard.

3. Press Ctrl+C or click the Copy button, which appears in the Standard toolbar of all the Office programs.

4. Switch to the program into which you want to embed the object. If the program isn't already running, start it by switching to Program Manager and double-clicking its icon. If the file into which you want the data copied isn't already open, open it.

5. Position the insertion point where you want the embedded object to appear.

6. Call up the <u>E</u>dit⇨Paste <u>S</u>pecial command to summon the Paste Special dialog box:

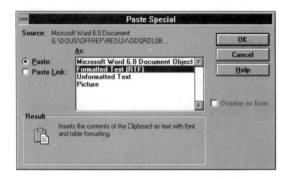

7. The Paste Special dialog box lists the various forms in which you can paste the contents of the Clipboard. Pick the one that includes the word *Object*. For example, to embed a Word document, choose Microsoft Word 6.0 Document Object.

8. Click OK.

Creating a New OLE Object

To create a new OLE object, follow this procedure:

1. In the program and file into which you want to embed the object, position the insertion point where you want the embedded object to appear.

2. Call up the Insert⇨<u>O</u>bject command to summon the Object dialog box.

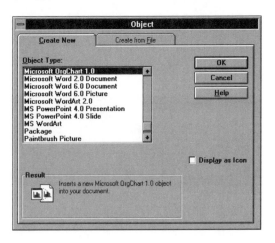

3. Make sure that the Create New tab is selected. If it isn't, click it.

4. The Object dialog box lists the various types of objects that you can create. Pick the type of object you want to create. For example, to create an OrgChart object, choose Microsoft OrgChart 1.0.

5. Click OK.

Inserting a File as an OLE Object

To insert an existing file as an embedded OLE object, follow this procedure:

1. In the program and file into which you want the existing file inserted, position the insertion point where you want the embedded object to appear.

2. Call up the Insert⇨Object command to summon the Object dialog box.

3. Click the Create from File tab.

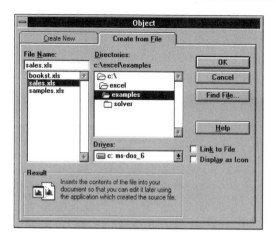

4. Select the file you want to embed. You may have to rummage about the disk a bit to locate the file.

5. Click OK. The file is inserted as an object.

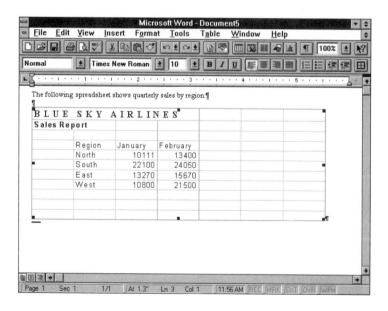

Inserting Objects by Dragon Dropping

Word, Excel, and PowerPoint support an editing technique called *drag and drop* (more affectionately known as *dragon drop*), which lets you copy or move text by dragging it with the mouse. You can also use dragon dropping to move or copy text from one Office application to another to create an embedded object. Here's the procedure:

1. Arrange your windows so that the program that contains the data you want to copy or move as an object and the program in which you want to embed the object are both visible:

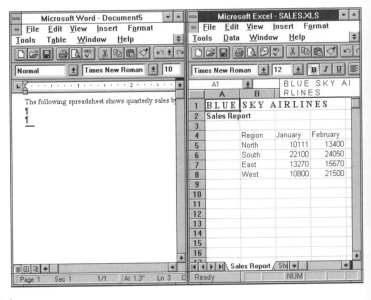

To quickly arrange all open windows, press Ctrl+Esc to bring up the task list and then click <u>T</u>ile.

2. Select the data that you want copied or moved:

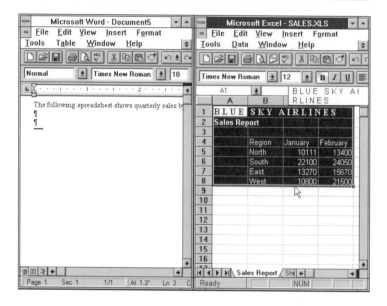

3. If you want to copy rather than move data with dragon drop, press and hold Ctrl.

4. Point the mouse pointer at the selection (in Excel, point at the border of the selection) and then press and hold the mouse button.

5. Drag the mouse to move the selection to the program in which you want to embed the object:

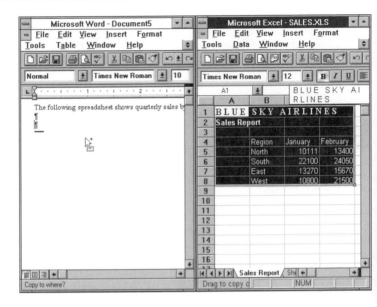

6. Move the mouse to the location at which you want the object embedded and then release the mouse button. (Release the Ctrl key too, if you're holding it.) The information is copied or moved.

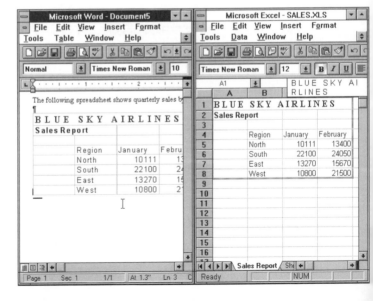

Note that simple text copied or moved in this way is pasted as text rather than inserted as an object. An object is inserted whenever you attempt to move or copy data that cannot be directly edited by the program to which you move or copy the data — for example, if you move or copy a range of worksheet cells to a Word document.

Editing an OLE Object

The two ways to edit an embedded OLE object are as follows:

- Double-click the object.
- Click the object to select it and then choose the Edit⇨ Object command.

When you edit an OLE 1 object, the program that created the object is called forward and appears in its own window.

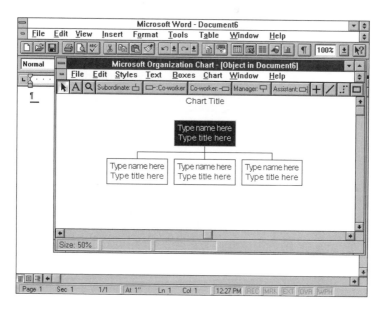

You can edit the object any way you want. After you're finished, choose File⇨Exit.

When you edit an OLE 2 object, the program that created the object takes over the program in which the object is embedded, replacing the original program's menus and toolbars with its own:

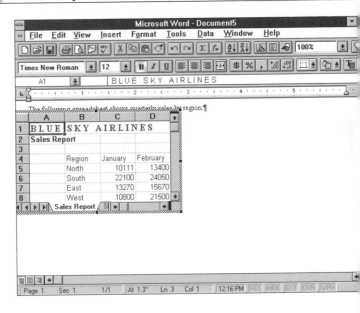

After you're finished, click anywhere outside the object's boundaries.

Deleting an OLE Object

To delete an embedded object, click it to select it and then press
Delete.

Sharing Information between Word and Excel

Office includes several features that are specifically designed to
allow you to exchange information between Word and Excel.

Exchanging Tables between Word and Excel

When you copy or cut a range of cells from an Excel worksheet
and paste it into Word, the worksheet data automatically con-

verts to a Word table. If the Excel worksheet includes formulas, the formulas' calculated values are pasted into Word.

Likewise, when you copy or cut a Word table to the Clipboard and then paste it into Excel, the table data automatically converts to worksheet cells.

Inserting an Excel Worksheet in a Word Document

To insert an empty Excel worksheet object into a Word document, follow this procedure:

1. Position the insertion point in the Word document at the place where you want the worksheet inserted.

2. Click the Insert Microsoft Excel Worksheet button in the Standard toolbar.

3. Hold down the mouse button and drag to indicate the size of the worksheet that you want to insert:

4. Release the mouse button, and the worksheet is inserted into Word:

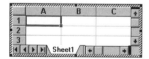

5. Edit the worksheet any way you want, inserting whatever cell values and formulas you need.

6. When you're finished editing the worksheet, click anywhere outside the worksheet. Word returns to its normal display:

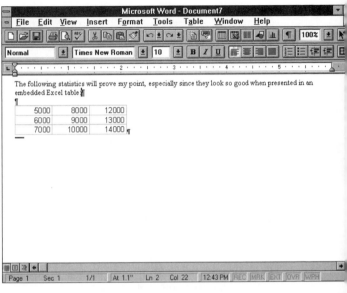

Using Excel Data in Mail Merge

Office provides three places to store the names and addresses for Word's mail merge feature: a Word table, an Excel worksheet, and an Access table. To use an Excel worksheet as a mail merge data source, follow this procedure:

1. In Excel, create a worksheet that contains the names and addresses to which you want to mail. The database should be kept in a range of cells with one row for each record and one column for each field — such as First Name, Last Name, Address, City, State, Zip Code. Here is an example of an Excel worksheet:

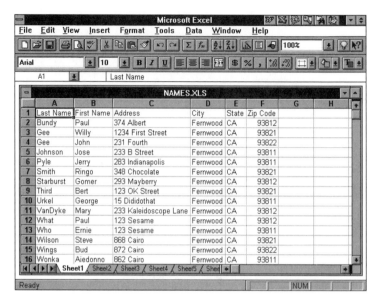

2. Save the file, exit Excel, and switch to Word.

3. Call up the Tools⇨Mail Merge command. The Mail Merge Helper dialog box appears.

4. Click the Create button to create the main document. Choose Form Letters and then select New Main Document to type a new letter.

5. Click the Get Data button and then select the Open Data Source option.

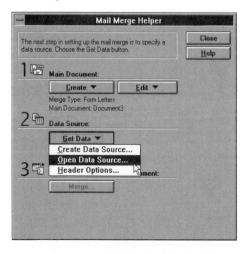

6. The Open Data Source dialog box appears:

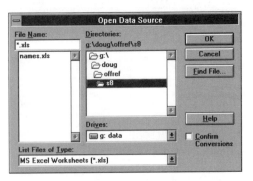

7. Select MS Excel Worksheet (*.xls) for the file type, find your file, and then click OK. Word asks whether you want to include the entire spreadsheet or just a range of cells:

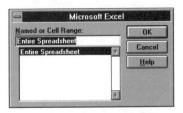

8. Click OK to include the entire worksheet. Mail Merge informs you that your main document doesn't contain any merge fields:

9. Click Edit Main Document. You are taken to the main document window with the Mail Merge toolbar visible. Type your letter, clicking the Insert Merge Field button whenever you want a merge field to appear.

10. To merge your letters, call up the Tools⇨Mail Merge command to summon the Mail Merge Helper dialog box. Click the Merge button to bring up the Merge dialog box. Finally, click the Merge button to merge the letters. A new document is created to hold the merge letters.

Sharing Information between Word and PowerPoint

Other than copying text and graphics via the Clipboard, several specific Office features are designed to share data between Word and PowerPoint. These features are covered in the following sections.

Using Report-It

The Report-It feature converts a PowerPoint presentation to a word processing document stored in RTF format. Although RTF isn't Word's native document format, Word can open and edit RTF documents. And you can use Word to convert the RTF document to a Word document if you want.

Here's the procedure for using Report-It:

1. In PowerPoint, open the presentation you want to convert.

2. Click the Report-It button.

3. PowerPoint launches Word and inserts the text from your presentation into Word as an outline:

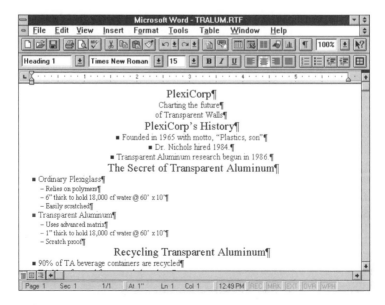

4. In Word, choose File⇨Save if you want to save the file.

Inserting a Word Outline in PowerPoint

You can convert a Word document to a PowerPoint presentation provided that the Word document uses standard heading styles to indicate its outline. Here's the procedure:

1. In PowerPoint, create a new presentation or open an existing presentation into which you want the outline inserted.

2. Call up the Insert⇨Slides command from outline view.

3. Pick the document file that contains the outline you want converted and then click OK.

4. Wait. If the document is big, this process can take a few minutes.

5. Behold the document converted to a presentation. Here's what the document file for this chapter looks like when converted to a presentation and shown in PowerPoint's outline view:

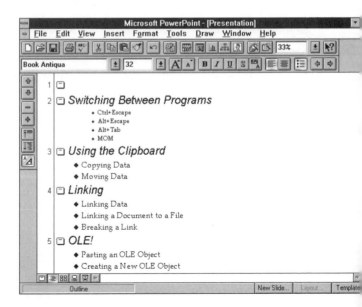

Creating a Word Table in a PowerPoint Presentation

To insert an empty Word table into a PowerPoint presentation, follow this procedure:

1. In PowerPoint, move to the slide where you want the table inserted.

2. Click the Insert Microsoft Word Table button in the Standard toolbar.

3. Hold down the mouse button and drag to indicate the size of the table that you want to insert.

4. Release the mouse button. The table is inserted into PowerPoint:

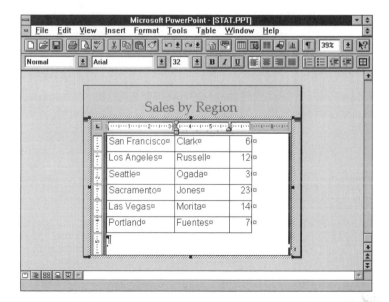

5. Edit the table any way you want, inserting any values and applying any formats.

6. After you finish editing the table, click anywhere outside the table. PowerPoint returns to its normal appearance.

To edit the table later, just double-click it.

Sharing Information between PowerPoint and Excel

PowerPoint allows you to insert Excel worksheet data directly into a slide.

Creating an Excel Worksheet in a PowerPoint Presentation

To insert an empty Excel worksheet into a PowerPoint presentation, follow this procedure:

1. In PowerPoint, move to the slide in which you want to insert the worksheet.

 2. Click the Insert Microsoft Excel Worksheet button in the Standard toolbar.

3. Hold down the mouse button and drag to indicate the size of the worksheet you want to insert:

4. Release the mouse button. The worksheet is inserted into PowerPoint.

5. Edit the worksheet any way you want. All of Excel's functions and formatting options are available.

6. When you're finished editing the worksheet, click anywhere outside the worksheet. PowerPoint returns to its normal appearance.

To edit the worksheet later, just double-click it.

Sharing Information between Word and Access

The most useful way to work with Access data from Word is to use Access as the data source for a mail merge. You can also insert Access data into a Word table.

Using Access Data in a Mail Merge

There are two ways to use Access data in a mail merge. The first, described here, is to use Word's Mail Merge Helper to use an Access database as the mail merge data source. The second, described later in this part, is to use Access' Mail Merge Wizard to export Access data to Word.

Here's the procedure for using Access data in a Word mail merge:

1. In Access, create a database that contains names and addresses. Use whatever field names you want: FirstName, LastName, Address, City, State, and ZipCode seem likely candidates.

2. Save the file, exit Access, and switch to Word.

3. Call up the <u>T</u>ools⇨Mail Me<u>r</u>ge command. The Mail Merge Helper dialog box appears.

4. Click the <u>C</u>reate button to create the main document. Pick Form <u>L</u>etters and then select <u>N</u>ew Main Document to type a new letter.

5. Click the <u>G</u>et Data button and then select the <u>O</u>pen Data Source option. The Open Data Source dialog box appears:

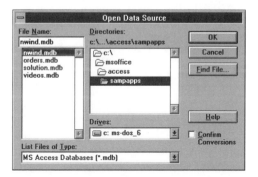

6. Select MS Access Databases (*.mdb) for the file type, find your file, and then click OK.

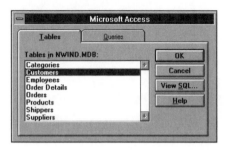

7. Pick the table you want and then click OK. Mail Merge informs you that your main document doesn't contain any merge fields.

8. Click Edit Main Document. You are taken to the main document window with the Mail Merge toolbar visible. Type your letter, clicking the Insert Merge Field button wherever you want a merge field to appear.

9. To merge your letters, call up the Tools⇨Mail Merge command to bring forth the Mail Merge Helper dialog box. Click the Merge button to bring up the Merge dialog box. Finally, click the Merge button to merge the letters. A new document is created to hold the merge letters.

Inserting Access Data into a Word Table

To copy data from an Access database into a Word table, follow this procedure:

1. In Word, call up the Insert⇨Database command. The Database dialog box appears.

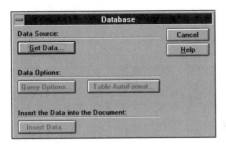

2. Click the Get Data button. The Open Data Source dialog box appears:

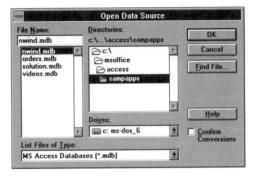

3. Select MS Access Databases (*.mdb) for the file type, find your file, and then click OK.

4. Pick the table you want and then click OK. You return to the Database dialog box.

5. Click Insert Data. The Insert Data dialog box appears.

6. Click OK. The data is inserted into a table.

You may notice that the table columns are too narrow to accommodate the data that's stored. The table looks like it's jumbled up, but the data is actually stored in the table correctly. If you want, you can adjust the column widths to give the table a neater appearance.

Sharing Access Data with Excel and Word

Access has several features specially designed to share data with other Office applications. The following sections describe some of these features.

Converting Access Data to Excel

You can easily convert an Access database table to an Excel worksheet by following this procedure:

1. In Access, open the database that contains the table that you want to convert to Excel.

2. Select the table or query that you want to convert to Excel.

 3. Click the Analyze It with MS Excel button.

4. Watch as Access converts the data to an Excel worksheet and then launches Excel and opens the newly created file.

Using the Merge It Wizard

The Merge It Wizard provides an easy way to use Access data in a Word mail merge. Just follow these steps:

1. In Access, open the database that contains the table that you want to use in a mail merge.

2. Select the table or query that you want to convert as the mail merge data source.

 3. Click the Merge It button. The Microsoft Word Mail Merge Wizard dialog box appears.

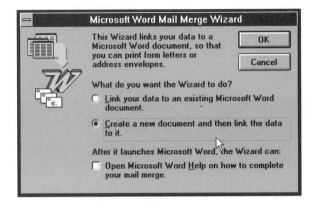

4. If the letter that you want to use for the mail merge already exists, select the Link, click OK, select the document, and then click OK again. If you haven't yet created the document, select Create and click OK.

5. Watch as Access launches Word and exports database data into the mail merge data source ready to be merged with the main document.

See Part II for more information about Mail Merge.

Index

• *N* •

• *O* •

• P •

• *T* •